LIGHTHOUSES
and LEGENDS
of the HUDSON

Saugerties Lighthouse (View across Hudson River
from Glunt Homestead)

LIGHTHOUSES
and
LEGENDS
of the
Hudson

Ruth R. Glunt

Library Research Associates, Inc.
Monroe, New York
1990

LRA Inc.
Library Research Associates, Inc.
Dunderberg Road, RD#6-Box 41
Monroe, New York 10950

Library of Congress Cataloging-in-Publication Data:

Glunt, Ruth Reynolds. b.1891- d.1979
  Lighthouses and Legends of the Hudson.
    Includes index.
    1. Lighthouses -- New York (State) -- Hudson River -- History.
    2. Hudson Valley -- History
    I. Title.
VK1024.N7G48   387   74-84583
ISBN:0-912526-14-9   CIP

Dedicated to my Husband
CHESTER B. GLUNT,
*who for twenty-eight years was in charge
of the U.S. Coast Guard
Light Attendant Station
Turkey Point, Saugerties, N.Y.*

Preface

Although their demise was comparatively re-
cent, the lighthouses of the Hudson River seem to
hark back to an era as remote and pleasant as an
actual lighthouse existence of perhaps a century
ago. Here in mankind's nearest equivalent to an
ivory tower, one might enjoy peace and splendid
isolation that was comforting but not hermitlike, for
past the front door went the great and fascinating
water traffic of bygone years. There were marine
craft of all types—the sloops and schooners, themselves inevitably giving way to progress; the big,
lumbering sidewheel towing steamers and then the
smaller propeller tugboats, with long tows of barges
and canalboats stretched out astern; the mighty
and beautiful passenger steamboats that grew and

grew until they could carry a small army in one passage.

The lighthouses had a front-row seat for this pageant of marine history, and at the same time they prevented much tragic marine history by warding off countless accidents. That was their mission, and they performed their mission well.

In the less distant past, the lighthouses saw a great change in the traffic on the Hudson. The steamboats became almost extinct; huge seagoing tankers and big freighters moved up and down a deepened river. This change came about through strides in scientific advancement and the advance eventually decreed that it was superfluous to maintain a whole house, with people living inside and with a big light on top, as a navigational aid on an inland river. So the little ivory towers were whisked away. At least in the log of one of them, long ago in 1910, the ever increasing tempo in technological advance was recorded when the keeper at Esopus Meadows Lighthouse set down, without a worry for grammar, "Aeroplane (Air Ship) passed down about 8:10 A.M. on W side of Light passed down the river out of sight." Little did the keeper know that the "Air Ship" was the harbinger of a new way of life that would cast him and his kind forever into limbo.

We who remember even dimly the days when a keeper would come out of his front door to wave a welcome at the first trip of a particular steamboat, or who rang his fogbell in melancholy farewell at the last trip of the season, can at least rest a little easier with the publication of this book by Ruth Reynolds Glunt, for herein the story of the Hudson

River lighthouses is kept bright for all who shape their course this way.

For many a year Mrs. Glunt has been collecting pictures and data in an area in which, for good reason, she is paramount. Her husband served the Government in the field of navigational aids; her attractive home is within pebble-skipping distance of the Hudson River; her primary interest beyond her family is the river and its history. Consequently, Mrs. Glunt, by both inclination and situation, has been in a position over the years to come by much more material than the ordinary mortal, and she has made the most of it.

Loyal followers of the Hudson will be deeply grateful for her efforts. The anecdotes stem from firsthand sources; the facts come from Government records; the pictures speak for themselves. So, as we read this book, we are in effect in Mrs. Glunt's cozy living room on a cold winter's night, with the wind whistling over the ice-covered river as she tells us of happenings near and dear to her heart, and to the heart of anyone who has ever ventured into the world of the rivermen.

Donald C. Ringwald

ALBANY, NEW YORK

Contents

Preface   vii
Introduction   xiii

LIGHTHOUSES

An Old Lighthouse Flag   3
Aids to Navigation   5
The Nine Lighthouses   12

LEGENDS

Ferries at Saugerties   79
The Old Wreck   86
Esopus Creek: Past and Present   89
Heaven at Krum Elbow   92
From Old Lighthouse Records   95
A True Conservationist   97
Old Overlook Tales   100

Fishing on the Hudson   110
Our Nautical Highway   115
Winter on the Hudson   122
The Tram Way   127
Who Lived Here?   131
Our Island   135

Acknowledgments   148
Picture Credits   149
Index   151

Introduction

Much has been written about the Hudson River; its beauty, history, and old estates. Lately, we hear much of its pollution and the neglect of its shorelines. This little book is a tribute to its Lighthouses and their functions because they are all of the past. Some have already been torn down and others are doomed, neglected, decaying and vandalized. Little Tarrytown, alone, seems in good hands.

The sloops, nightboats, the river pleasure steamers that carried thousands each summer to the mountains are all gone. The fishermen's nets and the long strings of barges with their families on board are no more.

Now the River is dredged regularly for large tankers and freighters from foreign ports; huge cement barges load at plants that have stacks belching out clouds of noxious smoke, and tall towers take the place of the Lighthouses.

Hundreds of pleasure craft race back and forth; mostly just for the sport of speed or noise. The occasional sailboat is a welcome sight, but has its traffic hazards these days. Maybe the future will improve the River if enough of the younger generation are interested.

LIGHTHOUSES

An Old Lighthouse Flag

Recently, an old flag was given me by a man who had been with the old U. S. Lighthouse Service for many years and later with the U. S. Coast Guard when the lighthouses came under their control.

My husband and I had never seen or heard of such a flag before, but many years ago it seems all lighthouses were supplied with them to fly on special occasions. Very few, if any, are still in existence.

This flag of heavy bunting measures two and one half by four feet. The tower is navy blue on a white ground with a bright red border. I treasure it among my box of lighthouse keepsakes.

Aids to Navigation

Aids to navigation really started with the Indians. They bent limbs of trees to point the route, made stone piles, signal fires, drove stakes in shallow flats, and likely had other signals to show where to travel by water. Later, sailing ships hung lanterns from poles, marked danger spots with stakes, and used an echo from rocky cliffs in fog or if caught out after dark. They usually dropped the hook by sundown, but they were often aground. The river has a three to four foot tide as far as Albany. Often sudden changes in the wind can buck or add to the flow of the tide.

The U. S. Lighthouse Establishment, in 1789, hired lamplighters who lived nearby danger spots, to hang lanterns on trees or posts. They furnished small wooden houses for oil, wicks, and supplies.

Stony Point Light, 1826

There were no lights during ice conditions of course, and often these little houses were washed away each spring.

The government built the first lighthouse on the river at Stony Point in 1826. It was never a dwelling, and has been left as a tourist attraction, high on a cliff in a state park.

The keepers' house was torn down and the W. P. A. built a handsome stone house in 1938 for a keeper. There is an automatic light and fog bell on the rocks below that can be turned on from the house if necessary. Here the keeper lives with his family in privacy with a view a millionaire could envy.

Keeper's House, U. S. Coast Guard, Stony Point

There were nine lighthouses originally built by the Lighthouse Establishment, which became the U. S. Lighthouse Service. Several small buildings were erected at dangerous places, but they were not family stations. The U. S. Lighthouse Service bought an old house at Four Mile Point, near Athens, and improved it for a keeper and family. In 1939, the U. S. Coast Guard took over this service and it became military, except for a few civilians still on the job.

Four Mile Point Light

Four Mile Point Dwelling

The lights originally were run on whale oil, then coal oil, and some by a high grade kerosene, that with a mantle, made an incandescent light called I.O.V., and finally electricity. These were the lighthouses, but the beacons were run by tanks of acetylene gas and later batteries; possibly, soon by atomic power. Where shore current was not possible for lighthouses, they had a battery standby system in case of power failure. The light was a small power bulb inside a cut glass lens that magnified the range. The old lenses were made in France, cut like diamonds and handsome when lit or even in sunshine. The keepers had orders to pull down the shades in the daytime; always light up a half hour

Fresnel Lense

before sundown and extinguish half hour before sunrise. "Never let the light go out" at night. NO excuse permitted for this; better to use an old oil lamp or even a large candle than no light. Some men had a bell rigged up to call them if they slept. Others climbed the steps often to check. There was a long wooden shaft outside on some houses from deck to roof that contained a weight, like on a cuckoo clock, that the keeper pulled up if foggy, to run the fog bell. After eight hours the heavy weight had to be rewound. Now, the fog bells are automatic, being turned on from shore; one at Danskammer was activated by a ship blowing its whistle and the bell answered. This has been discontinued as usually "out of order", or the batteries run down. A plane flying low overhead or a train on the West Shore could start it.

The Nine Lighthouses

The nine lighthouses were as follows:

1) Stuyvesant (called by some Upper Kinderhook) built in 1829 on the East Shore;

2) Coxsackie, built in 1830 on the West Shore;

3) Hudson City, built in 1874 in mid-channel;

4) Saugerties, 1835, on the West Shore, was rebuilt in 1869;

5) Kingston (Rondout), 1880, a handsome house on the West Shore, was torn down after a new lighthouse was built in 1913, nearer the channel;

6) Esopus Meadows, in mid-river, was built in 1839, rebuilt in 1872;

7) Stony Point, on the West Shore, was not a dwelling, and a steel tower was built in 1927;

8) Rockland Lake, 1894, near the West Shore;

9) Tarrytown, 1883, near the East Shore.

These dates are from the U. S. Coast Guard Light List, which has a few errors. The old Kingston Lighthouse was built in 1867 as Miss Cora Rightmeyer, now 93 of Kingston, has a record of being born there. The Stuyvesant Lighthouse listed as 1829, must have been replaced with a much larger building as the cornerstone with 1868 cut in the large block still lies on the shore, too heavy for a collector to move. Nearby, a huge clump of lilacs bloom each spring, planted by some keeper's wife. Four Mile Point built in 1831 on the West Shore was only a round tower, not a family dwelling.

Stuyvesant Lighthouse

The old Hudson River Lighthouses were called family stations and were home to some keepers for

Stuyvesant Lighthouse

years. One, at Stuyvesant, was about eighteen miles south of Albany along the East Shore. It was a huge dwelling, strongly built in 1868, and torn down in 1933, but closed long before when dredging changed

Stuyvesant Lense

the course of the Channel and a lighted tower was placed elsewhere. It was a desirable station, with a small foot bridge to the shore and enough ground for a garden, flowers, and a beach that was very popular in summer. Mr. and Mrs. Ed McAllister lived there for years, and although they had no children, they welcomed those of the neighbors who loved his parrot, pony and dog, and played on the upper deck with a watchful eye for a government boat with an inspector aboard. Then they would quickly leave for home.

The McAllisters were musical and took part in all community affairs and are still remembered by some of the Old Timers.

Many keepers under the lighthouse service had been on off shore stations for years, often miles from land in hazardous locations. The family rarely got on solid ground. In some cases, if there were children of school age, they either boarded on shore, or in winter the keeper stayed alone, while his family lived on land. Mail and supplies were brought to him by ship, and that not too often in bad weather. To be transferred to a place like Stuyvesant lighthouse, was considered a reward for years of duty and duly appreciated by a family man.

Stuyvesant's last keeper was Mr. Reilly. This was the only river lighthouse one could drive to from shore. When torn down in 1933, the huge foundation stones were moved for the base of the porch of the Stuyvesant Post Office.

Coxsackie Lighthouse

Coxsackie Lighthouse

Coxsackie's last civilian keeper was Mr. Jerome MacDougal, but an enlisted man was there, a Mr. Mace, when the lighthouse was closed and torn down in 1939. Previously, Mr. William Hoose, born 1816, was keeper for 32 years, and his son, Frank Lester, followed for 18 more which was quite a family record. William's daughter, Emma, was born on the light in 1868.

Mr. Hoose was born May 18, 1816, and married Christian M. Parslow who was born January 1, 1828.

William Hoose

Christian Hoose

He had fiery red hair and whiskers. Many relatives still live in Coxsackie.

The Lighthouse was originally on a separate island, but dredging joined it to the lower part of Rattlesnake Island. This probably was the home of copperheads, not rattlesnakes. Many river areas were infested with copperheads years ago, and a few still show up here and there.

When the U. S. Coast Guard tore down the brick and stone building in the late 1930's, local people offered to buy the interior woodwork, which was in beautiful condition and rare in those days. The government's orders were to burn it all which sadly was done.

Four Mile Point

Four Mile Point with its round tower high on a cliff, had a separate small stone dwelling, originally built in the early 1800's by a retired sea captain. There is a rumor of buried treasure nearby as the captain was reported to have had contacts. The Lighthouse Service bought this and the land, and remodeled the stone house for a keeper. Some called the place "Paddock's Island" as a marsh was behind it. It was also listed as "Echo Hill" for the rocky cliff, said to be 100 feet high, was used by skippers to bounce back an echo at night or in high fog. The last keeper was Mr. Burke who moved out in 1921. The tower was torn down in 1928 when a steel tower was erected at water level. This interesting old dwelling was sold privately in 1931 with four acres of land.

Aids

The automatic beacons either on land or on rock bases in the river are run by shore current or batteries, and have a sun relay device, putting out the light at daybreak, and on at dusk; also a flasher, each differently timed to various seconds, which blinks the light on and off. The river chart lists each light's characteristics, color and time of flash, so boatmen can check their locations. Each beacon has a lamp changer, to flip up a new bulb if one burns out. These are also on the lighthouses which have an astronomical clock that adjusts to daylight saving time. There are many floating lighted buoys on the river which are lifted out in winter because ice would damage them. The red numbered nuns,

Green Flats Automatic Beacon

and black numbered cans, stay in position unless moved by ice or run down by a ship. Despite these aids, many ships go aground. The larger ships use radar or compass.

Hudson Lighthouse

Hudson City, next below the Four Mile Point Tower, was closed in 1954. A civilian on shore was paid to manipulate the fog bell and check the batteries. The last keeper, Mr. Ed Brunner, kept his family on shore, and he went out each night. A well-known commercial artist painted this lighthouse for a Saturday Evening Post cover and took a

Navigation Buoy

Dayline Excusions on the "Hendrick Hudson"

lot of artistic license with the building. He had the keeper's family pose there on the deck and added a few children.

Before the days of heavy river traffic, the Hudson froze solid with a few air holes or tide rips and a keeper could walk ashore, except for a few days in spring break-up, or when ice started to form, usually in December. There was much ice boating, sleighing, and ice skating, and many visited the lighthouses when they could walk the ice.

Now our Hudson is jammed with broken ice cakes and shipping goes through daily. We forget the old days when the Lighthouse Keepers turned off the lights each winter till spring, and the river was closed to navigation. Hundreds of men, boys,

Hudson City Lighthouse

"Eastwind" Breaking the ice

horses and some of the Keepers worked from dawn
till dark in a holiday atmosphere for a few months
in the winter when the Ice Harvest was on. We
forget the old ice boxes, with the ice wrapped in
newspaper to keep it from melting so fast and the
pan underneath, often overflowing on the floor. And
the old wagon, the driver looking for the sign in the
window stating the number of pounds needed, is
no more. The kids ran behind to snitch a sliver to
suck, while the patient horse wearing a straw hat
with slits for his ears stopped unattended at each
house. The ice man was a husky individual for it
took muscles to heft the ice from the rear step, sling
it up on the scales, and then over his shoulder, drip-
ping down his neck, as he climbed steep stairs to
city flats. We forget chipping ice for the crank ice
cream freezer or pitcher of lemonade.

23

The ice was pure in those days, or at least everyone thought so, and labor was cheap. A day's pay was $1.25 or $1.50 for cold dirty work on the river from dawn to dark. The huge ice houses, usually built of hemlock with double walls for better insulation, were spaced along both sides of the river, but the west bank seemed to be favored. The Mulford ice house at Glasco was the largest, being 800 feet long. Men who patched the roof said it was like a baseball field. It had ten elevators to load the ice into the storage rooms. Men in this area were paid with scrip and the company maintained its own store on the dock. Horses were shipped by boat from New York City for the season. A huge chest of silver dollars was sent up for the Hamburg House because the men would accept no other pay. This was kept under careful watch in warm quarters for the men complained if the metal coins were cold in their pants! The houses were damp and dark, and later on were used for mushroom growing.

The Knickerbocker Ice Co., the largest concern, owned many houses on the river. The one at Turkey Point in Ulster County had a boarding house for men and boys and large horse stables. The ice was packed in layers of sawdust and hay, with an eighteen inch base of sawdust first. This house is long gone, but the ground here is so impregnated with the sawdust between the rocks and rotting dock timbers that copperhead and black snakes winter here, crawling out on the U. S. Coast Guard concrete dock to sun and breed. They probably are found at similar old river sites.

Mulford Ice House

After apple picking was over and winter stopped the stone quarry work, as well as farming and shipping, men and boys who were eager to cut ice watched the thermometer. It had to be twenty-nine degrees, although it took much lower to make ten or twelve inches of ice. Cakes were usually marked 22 x 32 x 12. If snow came first, this was not so good for it had to be plowed. Some men had to walk miles from their homes to the river. Stout planks were laid over the tidal edge to get safely on the ice. Horses, with cleats on their shoes to keep them from slipping, had to be watched although they sometimes fell in and had to be hauled out with much effort and cussing. They were rugged too, with their heavy winter coats of fur. The men

Cutting Hudson River ice for storage

Clearing the ice for cutting

usually wore hobnailed boots, and some had grippers strapped to their thick shoes. A fire was always handy to warm wet, cold feet and hands. The horses dragged a cutter to mark off the cakes. Some men sawed, other floated cakes through the open lanes of water to the house where they were lifted to the conveyer. The men inside arranged and layered them with the sawdust and hay. At the end of this era, which started to wane around 1900 and ended about 1936, power saws were used, not horses.

On the river, as the spring break up permitted, barges were pushed by tugs to the icehouses, and cakes were loaded in the holds for shipping to the cities. Some ships carried ice to South America and the West Indies. If it was well packed and there

Ice House for storage

"Eastwind" Coast Guard ice breaker off Saugerties Lighthouse

was no unusual storm delay, they figured only a ten percent melt!

Electricity and pollution changed it all, but labor prices and the unions would have anyway. Men of these days were a hardy breed; our younger generation could not and would not take it. It meant six days of hard labor at low pay, which was often spent on Saturday night as they thawed out in the nearest saloon, to sleep it off on Sunday, before a repeat performance.

Ice cutting tools now are collectors' items, high in price and scarce. Torque bars, saws, planes, scrapers, and horseshoes are in demand. If the saws are rusty, and the handles on the pike poles are rotten, city buffs and dealers still buy them!

Saugerties Lighthouse

During the Hudson Champlain celebration in 1959, a large blue and orange billboard sign was erected out front of the Saugerties Lighthouse by a local committee, saying "Saugerties Celebrates 350 Years of River Travel." Ships at night turned their searchlights on it in curiosity. It was the only sign of this type on the river and permission had to be obtained from Washington, D. C., for its display.

Saugerties is the oldest lighthouse still standing, and unless some repairs are made very soon its days are numbered. The first dwelling in 1835 was replaced in 1869. It is the most easily reached by land at present. The list of keepers which follows is typical of other lighthouses; some short stays, some

Saugerties Light

Saugerties Lighthouse

long. Some women took over as keepers as a family affair. Pay was low, some started at $500.00 a year, and often they had to transport their own coal and stoves.

Keepers had their own furniture supplemented by government supplies and a boat. Usually, the houses were spick and span, and visitors were made welcome. Hot coffee and dry clothes were supplied for a boatman in trouble. Water was pumped from the river for general use, but rainwater stored in a cistern, either in the attic or the cellar, from drainage off the roof into the gutters. These had shutoffs to permit water to run overboard until clear before turning into the cistern. Orders were to clean these out annually. Oil lamps were used for years, and in fact, each keeper had to account in his log for each gill and each wick. Also he recorded weather, visitors, rescues, hours of fog and anything unusual. At one lighthouse, the permanent closing was protested by the nearby town's people who claimed the keeper was needed to assist small craft. His log showed very few rescues although he had many. He seldom wrote it down because of the red tape, and typing of many copies for headquarters. He just helped others and wanted no glory. Before electricity and a telephone were installed, this keeper arranged with a neighbor on shore to hoist a large white flag on a flagpole if he was wanted, either by an inspector or on the telephone, and he would

Taking Inventory

row ashore for the message or visitory. At night, a flashlight was used. He also planned to hang a sheet out of a bedroom window if he needed help. A lamp on the window sill at night meant trouble. The fog bell could be rung steadily in an emergency. This arrangement later paid off as one afternoon he had a bad hemorrhage, and his wife started the bell and hung out the sheet. A doctor was there soon by boat and saved him.

Shortly before the Saugerties Station was closed in 1954, it had been completely modernized; steam heat, plumbing, electricity, phone and a Monel metal sink. The tender also brought up a large deep freeze. The keeper painted the three large bedrooms upstairs a month before the station was closed. Mr. Ed Pastorini was the last keeper and there were tears in his eyes the morning he moved his family out. The tender arrived with order to tear out the plumbing, furnace, fixtures, etc., and

Saugerties Lighthouse closed

gallons of water were simply drained out on the hardwood floors; some had heavy battleship linoleum, and the water was left to lie there. Windows were boarded up tightly and with no ventilation or light, dampness and cold were disasterous, and vandals since have added to the damage.

The National Archives records of keepers only go to 1914, and Conrad Hawk, the last on that list for Saugerties, died in 1940. The following keepers are from a list from National Personal Records, St. Louis, Mo.

Cyrus L. Gray	B.M.1c,U.S.C.G.	1940
H. H. Carlson		1942
Harold Fischer	B.M.2c,U.S.C.G.	1943
Thomas Walker	B.M.1c,U.S.C.G.	1944
Edward Pastorini		1950

Saugerties Lighthouse closed in 1954

Each tug, passing a lighthouse, gave a friendly blast on its whistle to the keeper.

Like the lighthouses, the sloops, ice cutting, night boats, and the Day Line, commercial fishing is of the past on the Hudson River. It was a real business years ago carried on from father to son, and in certain locations, profitable. The old net house behind the Saugerties Lighthouse was a choice location and active for years.

Recently we bought this old place adjoining our Hudson River home and it involved much more than we expected. It had belonged to various

ACCOUNT of Oil, Wicks, and Chimneys expended daily at *Saugertics Post*   Light-*on Dike* in the month of *January* , 1892, and showing the time of lighting and extinguishing, and the length of time lighted each night.

DAY.	Time of lighting.		Time of extinguishing light.		Length of time lighted.		Daily quantity of oil consumed in Light-house or Light-vessel lamps.				Number of chimneys broken each night.	Inches of new wick expended.	Quantity of oil set aside for hand and house lamps.	REMARKS ON THE WEATHER. (Dry, damp, rainy, snowy, light wind, moderate breeze, fresh breeze, or gale, &c.)
	Hour.	Min.	Hour.	Min.	Hour.	Min.	Galls.	Qts.	Pints.	Gills.				
1	4	43	7	35	14	52			1	1				
2	4	44	7	35	14	51			1	1				
3	4	45	7	35	14	50			1	1				
4	4	46	7	35	14	49			1	1				
5	4	47	7	35	14	48			1	1				
6	*Seized on account of ice in the creek.*													
7														
8														
31														

Total quantity consumed in the lamp of the Light— *on dike* ....

Total quantity consumed this month for use in the dwelling-house or quarters, and other hand lamps ....

Total quantity expended this month ....

	GALLONS.	QUARTS.	PINTS.
		3	1/4
		3	1/4

James Crawley, Light-Keeper.

............................., Ass't Keeper.

Order of Lens *Tubular lantern* Kind of Light. *F. Red*
Number of Wicks in burner *one*   Diameter of outer burner ....

Written by me—

James Crawley
Keeper.

2-387

families of commercial fishermen as it had tide water on two sides of its two and one-half acres. The property included an old house and several other dilapidated buildings. One, a large barn-like structure close to the river edge, called the net house had many other uses. It faced a shallow flat curving in from the river channel with a three to four foot tide across wild grasses and river lilies. The original settlers lived entirely by fishing, plus a garden, and various fruit trees.

Many, many years ago, a stockade of wooden planks with a gate was built in the bay and sturgeon were driven inside and trapped. These were plentiful and called "Albany Beef" by some. Their steaks could be smoked, the roe sold at a good price and the rest of the fish made fine fertilizer. Often they weighed over 200 pounds, but are very rare now.

Later, nets were made and used in various ways and shad, carp, herring, bull-heads, eels, and occasionally smelts were caught. Snapping turtles, some 40 pounds, were caught and the meat used.

The fishermen dug out an inlet near the net house for a pond. They dammed it across so tide water entered over the dam and enough water remained until the next tide which kept their fish alive until sold. They also dug out and stoned up a slip to haul in a flat bottomed boat near a huge net reel. This was a large wooden frame with a wooden rack inside that could be turned around by a crank on the side. This rolled up the net directly from the boat. They usually marked the damaged places when rolling it wet, and later, at their leisure, mended the torn areas.

Capt. Eugene Coons, an old "Tug Boat" man

Net storage house

Carp were always put in the pond alive. Later a tank truck came from New York to keep them fresh until sold. Jewish custom demanded this and much gefullte fish in the cities came from this pond. A net haul ran 1500 pounds or more. The price back in the 1930's averaged 14 cents a pound at the pond.

The nets for these fish were staked out across a corner of the bay at high tide and the carp were trapped when the tide dropped. The men in hip boots could pick them up and throw them into flat-bottomed skiffs and dump them in the pond. Usually, there would be a few golden carp in the haul.

Fishing net on reel

These are beautiful, a real red-gold, often 8–12 inches long, and were in demand for park pools or on "them millionaires" estates, so-called by the fishermen.

The lighthouse keepers were always glad to have the various fishing seasons start. They knew all the local fishermen and often gave them a hand with a heavy drift of shad or their scap nets. In return, they would have fresh fish for dinner.

Shad were caught each Spring in drift nets in deep water, usually at the turn of the tide. Two row boats were used holding the net between them, the floats on the net drifting out in an arc. A passing ship could ruin a net, and the men had to work fast sometimes. It was rough hard work and few do it this way anymore. In fact, few men fish for carp now as there is no market.

Herring were another spring catch, usually later than the shad. The old way, called scapping consisted of a strong pole built into the bow of the skiff with a crank to raise and lower a baited net hooped to the top of the pole to scoop them up out of the water. This could also be done along the shore with a large dip net. Every family years ago had barrels of salt herring stacked away in the cellars for winter.

Long ago, eels were trapped in slatted wooden crates with a funnel-type entrance. These crates were lowered into water about 8–10 feet deep and tied to stakes. Later, metal traps were used with wire mesh sides as they were lighter to handle. Usually, these were baited with river mussels. A smaller trap was submerged to catch live bait or minnows, which had a good sale to trout and bass fishermen.

All this gear was kept in the net house plus much else that we found. It contained a small four-wheel open wagon for a man to pull walking inside the shafts. I have been told this made many a trip through the village streets, the wagon bed loaded with fresh fish to sell. (A boy with a small pony or burro would have been thrilled with this wagon! An antique collector took it.) The large flat bottomed row boats were stored winters in this building; repaired or painted, maybe even built

Claude, a Hudson River fisherman

there. On the walls hung old oil lanterns, muskrat traps and boards for drying their skins; even found an old bear trap. Large dip nets hung from the rafters. These were cleverly made from a strong forked branch, usually ash or hickory. The net inside the hoop would be approximately 30 inches across. There also was a hanging, much used, fish scale. A long work bench had bins above and below with old nails, bolts, etc., as well as two good wooden planes, handmade, and many old tools. A handmade wooden fid for rope work was smooth as silk. Also I found an old paint scraper, old handmade oars, boat hooks and stakes, besides a pike pole for ice walking. Kegs of lead sinkers were under the workbench—several sizes and some handmade of melted lead. There were several blue stone anchors with a drilled hole and iron ring. An old wooden affair on the wall confused us, but we now think it was to shell hulls off walnuts or butternuts, as it has holes of several sizes. Also there was a treadle grindstone.

The back of the building had stairs to a loft where nets could be stretched across the rafters and there were several fyke nets up there with their wooden hoops. These were staked underwater—even under ice in winter. The hoops formed a series of traps for fish. The floor in the loft was covered with wooden and cork floats for the carp nets. Flat boards (buoys) were used for the shad nets. I shoveled a lot of the floats into baskets to save. Many were handmade from a block of wood with an augur drilled hole, then whittled or sanded to shape. Some were stained a dull red or blue. The cork floats were rotted.

One day, I returned from town to find my husband had opened a door in the loft and shoveled the floats down in the water below. The bay for nearly half a mile out was full of bobbing net floats. He figured we had saved enough and the place really needed cleaning up. I called a neighbor who came with his station wagon and when the tide returned some of them, he shoveled what he wanted into his car. Later, he attended a sale of antiques and told my husband he saw similar floats valued at two dollars each!

Coast Guard tender at Turkey Point Base

Turkey Point Dock

In winter, nets could be knit in the old building. A strong linen thread was used then although nylon is used now. The needle was similar to a tatting hook, only larger, and I found several, some bone, some wood. This was also a wonderful workshop for any winter project, as the big doors faced south and the sun warmed the men sitting on the kegs or boxes swapping yarns as they knitted or mended nets. On occasion, when too much hard cider was around, the fishermen slept if off in the net house, rather than risk the rolling pin at the dwelling.

Now there is talk of trying to save this Saugerties light. In 1954, the Hudson River Conservation Society wrote many letters to department heads protesting the closing, and they were reassured it would be maintained as usual but made automatic.

But a leak in the slate roof stayed a leak. Lately, the Hudson River Valley Commission has made a complete survey of all remaining river lighthouses and submitted plans for them. But the delay over the years will add greatly to the cost if anything is ever done.

In 1938, the Coast Guard built a large, deep water concrete dock at Turkey Point about four miles from Saugerties on the West Shore. The warehouse and office serviced the whole area as ships left supplies on the dock. Buoys were painted and put in condition for spring. Now this is closed and deserted, and the copperhead snakes have taken over.

Under the Lighthouse Service, one man managed his area and duties alone although the work was often hazardous, especially in bad weather. My husband had much technical inspection to do and a large area to cover. If a light was reported out or improperly operating, he was ordered to attend at once. I often went along in his motor boat, rather than sit home and worry, so I would pack two sandwiches and put on foul weather gear. I was of some slight help at times rowing the skiff away from the rocks as a large ship passed when he was on a high tower to save him climbing down and back again.

Once at Greer Point (which President Roosevelt later changed with much publicity to "Crum Elbow" at Hyde Park), I walked up the wooded slope while my husband corrected the troubles at the light there. A stout man with a large cigar and a dog walked out of the woods near me and we had a

Aerial View of Turkey Point, U. S. Coast Guard Base

friendly chat as to where I came from, etc. Later, it occurred to me he greatly resembled Winston Churchill! Even an English manner of speech! As I was on Roosevelt property and Mr. Churchill visited there about this time, I likely interrupted his walk!

We had experiences of bad storms and some incidents. Once, a small boy was sighted adrift in mid-channel in a rubber tube. He was unconcerned; just drifted away while swimming but had gone many miles before we picked him up. He little realized that an old rubber tube is hardly reliable!

45

Small boats often needed a tow; lacked gas or had engine trouble.

One morning with zero temperatures, an order came to relight a tower in mid-channel. Ice prevented using a boat and a drive of several miles by car was needed to reach the area which was between towns and isolated. I went along and sat in the car quite upset, while my husband walked the ice to the tower over deep water. He carried a long pole, but the icebreaker had gone through the day before, and the ice had many cracks. I tried to figure out my nearest help if he went through! He made it safely, although a bit wet and very cold. Luckily, I had a thermos of coffee and a bottle of brandy along!

◀*Turkey Point Beacon Light*

Turkey Point Base

After the U. S. C. G. took over the Lighthouses and the river work, several enlisted men were assigned to his station here at Turkey Point, and I went no more. Women were banned; although orders for enlisted personnel stated always two men in a boat for safety. A civilian was not so ordered—and if his men were on liberty or unavailable, and the call urgent, the civilian still went alone.

One early evening my husband noticed that the light on the lighthouse near us was not on an hour before sundown. He knew the keeper's wife was away visiting her folks and that Joe was likely to celebrate uptown with the boys while he had the chance. So he walked over to the keeper's garage, to find his car there and the garage locked. He went across the road to the dock where the keeper moored his skiff and found it poorly tied to the ladder. One oar was missing and the box of groceries were strewn on the dock and milk bottles broken in the boat.

He feared Joe had fallen overboard and as nearly dark by then flashed his light down into the water, alarmed he might have drowned. With no other signs he started out through the woods toward the lighthouse and found Joe's shoes and pants scattered in the muddy path where he had fallen many times. Relieved that he was safe, he continued on only to see the light come on as he neared the swelling. When he entered the kitchen, Joe came staggering down from the tower, plastered with mud. "Don't turn me in, chief," he said. "I'm o.k. I'm not drunk, chief. She's lit. I made it."

The Lighthouse keepers and their families usually stopped what they were doing when they heard the slap of the paddle wheel and the whistle of the Day Line Boat. "Here she comes" meant getting out on the deck to wave and ringing the fog bell. The new flag went up each year on the pole at the station when the Day Line season started, and the torn old one that had flown daily had to be turned in for survey before a new one could be issued.

Dayliner "Peter Stuyvesant"

Watches could usually be set by the passing steamer unless a storm or unusual tide had delayed the ship. At Saugerties, the down boat passed at noon, and the up boat at 3 p.m.

The Hudson River Day Line started in 1863 and stopped service to the upper river in 1949 although continued to Bear Mt. and turned at Poughkeepsie. But its days are numbered! Only one ship, the Alexander Hamilton, is left of their seven steamers. The favorite was the Robert Fulton; her whistle was like music to the river folk. Children called her the up and down boat because of her walking beam.

I remember hearing the ships nearing Saugerties suddenly blast on their loudspeakers, "Ladies and Gentlemen, you are now approaching the Saugerties Lighthouse, at the mouth of the beautiful Esopus Creek. The village of Tivoli is opposite." Then the band would play louder and the whistle

Dayliner "Robert Fulton"

would salute the keeper as he waved and rang the bell. But he would rush quickly to his skiff tied alongside the ladder, to hold it off before the large swells rolled in and over his dock. The Day Line rollers were often a hazard to small boats. But venturesome young folks thrilled to ride the swells and hung around in small craft waiting for the ship to pass to head into the waves.

Sometimes they miscalculated and the keeper had to make a rescue. The stunt was dangerous and frowned on by the Captain of the ship.

Kingston Lighthouse

The old lighthouse at Kingston, built in 1867, was a handsome stone building near the Rondout Creek mouth. It was abandoned in 1913 and later torn down when a new one was built nearer the channel after the Creek was dredged and diked. The Murdocks were keepers at both stations, but Mr. Howard later was hurt on a fall on the ice and after that Coast Guard men were there until it closed in 1954.

The last keeper, Chief Lange, was very popular locally and very capable. Many will remember the present Kingston Lighthouse as they used to pass it on the Rhinecliff-Kingston Ferry.

When a keeper at the Rondout Light was hurt by a fall on the ice and hospitalized, the U. S. Coast Guard New York office was notified by my husband to send up a relief man, and told that the keeper's wife and two daughters were still living there. The

Old Kingston Lighthouse

relief arrived one night—a nice looking enlisted colored boy, well mannered and his uniform immaculate, to report for duty. My husband took him out to the lighthouse reluctantly to have the door slammed in their faces. His orders had to be obeyed however, and New York was told of the situation, but refused to make any change. Needless to say, my husband had a problem of immediately moving out the family to shore, bag and baggage, as the furniture was all theirs. And to make it worse, the temperature was near zero as they went over the ice. The Coast Guard said "no discrimination," but the lady said plenty!

Parlour in the Old Kingston Lighthouse

Esopus Meadows Lighthouse

Esopus Meadows, built in 1839, and rebuilt in 1872, is far out on the River with a large shallow flat to the West. It is told that years ago cows grazed on the meadows, but either nature or the wash of large ships has put it all under water at any tide. This light needs a foghorn or a bell, if any place does, but since closed in 1965 and made automatic, people on the shore complained if the bell rang too long as no one was there to turn it on and off so the bell is silent. Ice jammed against the heavy stone foundation years ago and it has a bad list. The log

Construction of Rondout Lighthouse in 1913

of a keeper reports several large barges in past storms jammed against it. A Spanish keeper long ago had a parrot who loved to chase a ball across the tilted floor. A log of several years is very amusing reading. Later on, a civilian keeper, John Kerr, had two deodorized skunks that ran around the deck at night. He also had a pet bantam rooster which sat in the bow of his rowboat when he went ashore and had a brief time to scratch on land. A small dog always sat in the stern with the keeper. When Mr.

Kerr and his wife moved out, three enlisted men were kept there for years until it closed.

Excerpts from a Hudson River Lighthouse Station Log

As Written by the Keeper

1879; Dec. 19: Eagale last trip down.

Dec. 20: M. Martens last trip down; Cornells last trip up.

Rondout Lighthouse completed

Dec. 21: James W. Baldwin last trip down. Therosameter 2 above zero at sunset.

1882; Mar. 2: Navigation open.

Mar. 27: Steamer Thomas Cornell Sunk. Rainy, south east wind.

Jul. 14: Southwest wind, Steamer Charlotte Vandervillte sunk.

1886; Mar. 15: Channel opened here today and the ice moved off the flats; 35 above zero.

Mar. 18: Navigation opened, the first boat with a tow up, Propeller A.C. Cheneye, 3 ice barges.

Mar. 20: First trip of City of Kingston up; first trip of Norwich down with a tow.

Mar. 22: First trip of L. D. Black.

Mar. 23: First sloop down.

May 22: First trip of Mary Powell.

May 29: First trip of Albany and Drew.

Jun. 2: Fresh breeze, south wind and rain; steamboat Jacob Leonard Sunk below the Island struck on the rocks.

Jun. 24: City of Kingston ran into the Schooner Mary Atwater in the Highlands and Sunk her; two lives lost.

1887; May 17: First trip of Steamer Mary Powell.

Oct. 17: Last trip of Mary Powell and Steamer New York.

Dec. 28: Navigation closed; 10 above zero.

1892; Jan. 3: First snow for season of 1892.

Jan. 11: Navigation on river closed.

Jan. 25: Knickerbocker commenced to work in ice.

Mar. 24: Navigation open, ice breaking up in channel.

Mar. 29: First tow up, Cheny ice barges.

Apr. 6: Heavy winds; full tides.

Apr. 11: Fishing season commencing.

Apr. 24: Dr. Kenedy aground at 5 in morning on Meadows; pulled off by I. M. North.

Apr. 27: Moved in light station; relieved Mr. Augustus York. Mr. J. J. Horan present. (Mr. George R. Humphrey now acting keeper).

1893; Mar. 13: Calm afternoon; fresh East wind by noon. Clear, warm and pleasant; no water on the ice. First trip of the Transport. At 4 p.m. ice moved out of the Rondout creek, taking with it 35 steam and canal boats.

1893; May 27: First up trip of the New York (Day Boat).

May 29: First up trip of the Albany (Day Boat).

Dec. 5: Last trip of Martin. George R. Humphrey, Jr., born 10 a.m. at this Lighthouse.

1899; May 3: A tow; tug, Geo. W. Washburn; struck the Esopus Meadows Lighthouse at 11 a.m.

1903; July 18: Steamer Central Hudson ran down sloop Contrivance and the master was drowned.

July 19: Martin Saunders put light at wreck of the sloop Contrivance before dark.

July 22: Martin Saunders put light at wreck before sunset but it was out at 8:15 p.m.

Aug. 5: U.S.L.H. tender Daisy went up at 4:25 p.m.

1903; Sep. 14: Inspected; Station in good condition, but lamps not cleaned and keeper absent from station and is evidently neglecting duty by being frequently absent. Dwelling needs painting. Keeper hereby directed to paint dwelling and admonished to be more attentive to duty or will probably be transferred to less desirable station or discharge.

Oct. 3: Mr. Humphrey resigned and left station. John T. Dixon in charge.

1904; Jan. 15: Keeper left station at 7 a.m. on so day's leave of absence. Mrs. J.T. Dixon took charge as act keeper.

Feb. 13: Keeper returned to Station at 6 p.m. after an absence of 28 days.

Nov. 6: Str Gardinia arrived 7:30 a.m. with Mr. Oliver from Romer Shoal.

7: Mr. Dickson former keeper left 12:06 p.m. resigned.

8: Mr. Oliver took charge of lights as keeper (Charles W. Oliver).

1905; Mar. 24: Str Norwich passed down river breaking ice followed by Str New York.

25: 1st Tow of Barges went down river today.

Oct. 21: Str N.Y. made last trip down.

23: Albany made last trip of season down.

1906; Jan. 3: Str Norwich & Bob went down with tow.

4: Str Norwich & Bob went back.

9: Norwich & 2 tugs passed down with tow of Ice.

10: Norwich returned.

28: Mr. Murdock called today.

May 15: Str New York made trip up river.

May 21: Str Mary Powell 1st trip.

Sep. 27: Str Mary Powell last trip.

Oct. 20: Str Albany made last trip of season.

22: Str N.Y. made last trip of season.

1907; Jan. 8: Str Rob passed up & down also 1 tow of barges

14–18: Wife şick with bad face.

19: Wife so sick had Tug boat Rob to bring Dr. Decker off to see her.

21: Wife still on sick list (River closed again).

May 11: Thomas J. Murray took charge of station as Keeper.

12: Mr. Chas. W. Oliver left this station at 7 a.m. to go to North Hook Beacon Light Station.

1908; Mar. 23: Tugboat Hercules went on mud flats N. of Light 4:30 p.m. about 1/2 mile. Tug pulled off 5 p.m. Cloudy to Rain & Fog light NE to SE wind.

In winter, many keepers moonlighted (a word unknown then) with a shore job; ice cutting when available or hauling wood to a sawmill or any handy job. Some men worked on the New York Central tracks. In summer, if all in order at their station and no inspectors due, they picked fruit nearby. Their pay was low under the Lighthouse Service and some had large families.

The keepers were usually early risers and their duties not difficult. They had to clean the many

Esopus Meadows Lighthouse

Supply sled

lamps and fill same; polish the brass daily called bright-work; wax floors and pump water as needed. The usual housework was done by his wife; also necessary to row ashore for mail and supplies. In

Mrs. John Kerr, keeper's wife, cleaning the lens

winter, they sledded a load over the ice, weather permitting. In good conditions, the womenfolk went along.

Of course, boats had to be kept painted (usually each Spring) and the picket fence around the deck repaired and painted. They usually rotated painting the rooms; one a year in bad weather, with a dreary color supplied by the service.

Some keepers liked to fish. One, I knew, painted pictures. Usually they had some hobby, rope work, carving decoy ducks or even knitting. No T.V. or radio in those days, but many had a phonograph— and most of them loved visitors.

Years ago, a lighthouse keeper's wife had a reputation for setting a good table despite a smoky coal range, no running water or electric refrigerator. True, she had an icebox as in winter a piece of ice could be chopped off the river ice right at the doorway. And when open water, the keeper could row to the nearest icehouse for a chunk, carefully wrapped in gunny sacks. On rare occasions frozen custard was made by chipping up the ice and hand cranking the tub freezer. This was usually a 4th of July event when company came.

Supplies were brought in by rowboat, or in winter, over the ice, with a wooden box nailed to the sled. Of course, this was usually a weekly affair, no daily trip. And in mid-winter, with hazardous ice conditions, often not even then, although the keeper tried to get his mail every few days.

I remember visiting a lighthouse when the keeper arrived by rowboat with his supplies in rough weather. After tying up his skiff, as he lifted

Aid in an emergency

his box of groceries across to the dock, the boat
lunged out, and it all went into the river. The apples
were salvaged quickly as they bobbed around, but
all the rest was a complete loss, except for a large
ham, which they finally hooked with a grapple.

In those days a barrel of flour and a barrel of
sugar was kept on hand; it was a hard job for the
man to handle, and get it aboard safely. A ten or
twenty pound tin of lard was kept in a cool corner
in the cellar. Crocks of homemade sauerkraut and
pickles were stored as well as jellies and jams that
were also homemade. Of course, there was always

63

a keg of vinegar, but hard cider was frowned on, but with a few raisins added, it was often available. Salted herring were usually put down each spring. These are still plentiful and easy to catch, but seldom relished these days. Potatoes and apples kept well in a cool corner of the cellar, but had to be protected from rats and mice; hams and slabs of bacon were hung up and watched carefully for rats are always around docks. Buckwheat and cornmeal flour for panny cakes were kept handy and maple syrup was cheaper in those days, but still a treat. Coffee was bought in the bean and hand-ground fresh. The delicious smell of the fresh coffee was seldom lacking. Coffee was always offered to visitors or inspectors with homemade cake and cookies. An inspector or workman sent up from New York for repair work always paid for his dinner, usually twenty-five cents. This was way back of course, but a Keeper's pay then was very low, and pennies counted.

Later when the lighthouses were electrified in the middle or late forties by a cable run from shore, other improvements were made. A telephone and ship to shore radio added increased duties, but it was very convenient to call for shore help at the New York office if supplies became very low in midwinter and no chance to get ashore. Then one of the tenders came with much needed groceries or could even pick up a doctor in an emergency. Two of the Hudson River Lighthouses were difficult to reach when ice conditions were not safe; Hudson and Esopus Meadows.

The keepers' living conditions had improved wonderfully from the early days of the River Lighthouses when the United States Coast Guard decided to close them all. They had even sent up huge deep freezers shortly before the families were moved out and the lighthouses were abandoned.

When the lighthouses were improved from the old style of heating by small stoves in a couple of the main rooms to modern steam heat by radiators, the usual allotment of five tons of coal was delivered in summer by a Coast Guard tender. As winter became severe, the five tons shrunk and the keeper gave ample notice of this lack of coal. But the government departments move slowly and he had to resort to wood before the Comanche, a large ice-breaker, arrived with an ample supply. The problem was to get it to the lighthouse; heavy ice and rocks made it impossible to moor alongside. The crew went overboard on the ice and sledded the coal in canvas bags to the gangplank, then formed a bucket brigade to pass it into the cellar coal chute.

Drinking water was always a problem to the keepers as they had a cistern with drains from the roof. In a dry spell or with careless usage, the tenders came with fresh water aboard and pumped it into the cistern by a huge hose. Sadly, sometimes the same hose had just supplied kerosene or oil to another station, and the drinking water had a not too pleasant smell or taste.

In the improvement plan of the lighthouses, the fresh water came from one faucet and the river

water from one next to it; identical. Often the river
water intake was only a few inches away from the

Stony Point

sewer outlet pipe, and the keeper soon learned to be careful.

One young enlisted fellow was ordered to take over for a civilian keeper on vacation and drank from the wrong faucet for a week or more before he complained of the taste and odor. The keeper had failed to brief him on such minor details. Luckily he had had his shots.

Stony Point

West Point had a small frame building for supplies, and a light tower on Flirtation Walk, but it was never a family dwelling, although a keeper lived nearby. Now there is just the steel tower.

Stony Point, next down the River, described earlier, is worth a visit through the historic State Park. There is a picnic area, fine museum and a beautiful view from the hill by the old tower, built on the same site, with stone from the old Fort, captured from the British by Mad Anthony Wayne in 1778.

Rockland Lake, years ago, had a round tank house with the light on top and a keeper and his family lived there, but this was torn down and a steel tower erected, not far from the West Shore. The Light List dates it from 1894 to 1923.

Rockland Lake Lighthouse

The following record from National Archives, Washington, D. C., on the Rockland Lake Lighthouse explains the leaning tower which was a local mystery.

1888; ROCKLAND LAKE, HUDSON RIVER, N.Y.

"There is a shoal known as Oyster Beds in the Hudson River about 28 miles above New York City, off the Rockland Lake Landing, which the Hudson River pilots and parties engaged in the business of transpor-

Rockland Lake, N.Y., Lighthouse

tation of passengers and freight ask to have marked by a light and fog signal. The old-fashioned side-wheel steamers engaged in the navigation of the Hudson River were light draught vessels and could pass over this shoal; but many of the new steamers are propellers, and are of such heavy draught that the shoal is dangerous to them. Steam vessels all lay their courses close to the Rockland Lake Landing.

If there were a light and fog signal on the shoal in question, they would, coming downstream and taking departure from Stony Point Light, lay their course direct for the new light until the Kingsland Point light became visible, which would indicate a turning point. These courses would be reversed in going upstream. In times of snow or fog, a signal would obviously be invaluable. From an examination recently made it has become evident that the safety of navigation requires that a light and fog signal should be established off Rockland Lake Landing, on the eastern end of the bank, where the Coast Guard chart gives nine and one-half feet of water. It is estimated that this can be done for $35,000, and the Board recommends that an appropriation of that amount be made for this purpose."

1895; ROCKLAND LAKE, HUDSON RIVER, N.Y.

"This work, which was done under contract, was finished September 12, 1894. The fog signal apparatus was not included in the contract, but as soon as practicable this part of the work will also be finished. The station was lighted on October 1, 1894. A quantity of riprap was placed and an icebreaker was built to protect the pier.

1903; ROCKLAND LAKE, N.Y. From the Treasury Dept; to the Speaker of the House of Representatives:

This Department has the honor to state, at the instance of the Lighthouse Board, that the icebreaker which was built to protect the lighthouse at Rockland Lake, Hudson River, N.Y. is being continuously washed away, so that the lighthouse structure is dangerously exposed and needs more efficient protection.

The Rockland Lake lighthouse was built in 1894 and in the same year a riprap icebreaker or breakwater, was placed to protect the structure. Soon after its construction, the light tower began to lean in a direction nearly parallel to the breakwater, continuing this inclination until 1897, when the tower seems to have settled. The old icebreaker having now been so badly washed away that it is not deemed a safe protection for the lighthouse, it becomes necessary that some action be taken to improve the conditions.

The Lighthouse Board, at its session on April 7, 1902, considered this matter and concluded that the lighthouse in its present inclined position needs better protection, and that an icebreaker ought to be built in a somewhat different position from the old and deteriorated one, in order to relieve the pressure near the base of the cylinder and at the same time protect the tower from the heavy ice which every winter breaks in Haverstraw Bay and Hudson River and is forced against this tower. The Board estimates that this can be done for a cost not to exceed $6,450, and it earnestly recommends that an appropriation be made therefor.

This Department concurs with the Board in this matter, and therefore has the honor to ask that the proper measures be taken to include in the deficiency bill, that it may be made immediately available, an appropriation of $6,450 for building this proposed icebreaker at the Rockland Lake, Hudson River, N.Y. light station.

1906, ROCKLAND LAKE, NEW YORK

On January 22, 1906, contract was made for delivering and placing 3,000 tons of riprap stone as an icebreaker here. The work was done during April, a total of 2,972.2 tons having been delivered and placed. Various repairs were made."

Station closed permanently in 1923, and demolished.

Tarrytown Lighthouse

Tarrytown Light was erected 1881, lighted 1883, closed 1958. It is offshore 500 yards from Kingsland Point, East shore of Hudson River.

Tarrytown Lighthouse

The round house at Tarrytown, formerly called Kingsland Point, is larger than the one at Rockland Lake and was built near the East Shore in 1883. There is a round room on each floor. Two keepers had children who drowned there and a rule was made, no small children on lighthouses.

The light was eliminated when the Tappen Zee Bridge was built and the Westchester Historical Society is taking over the building. Just a year or so before it was closed, Ed Murrow of *Person to Person* filmed the lighthouse for T.V. He came up with a large crew, two days ahead, and set it up; fresh flowers, and the Coast Guard man briefed to wear his white uniform, and everything very fine for life on a lighthouse. The young fellow and his wife were overly enthusiastic of his career on the film, but a month or so after, when his enlistment was up he got out of service.

Mr. LeClerc was the last civilian keeper, followed by enlisted men stationed there until closed. Light could be seen for 14 miles (fresnel lense).

Race Day on the Hudson — Hellkat No. 3

The tank tower had three decks called boat, bell, and lantern decks. Keepers made many rescues of boatmen and swimmers from the wide Tappen Zee.

Last, the so-called little Red Lighthouse under Washington Bridge is well known, but was never a real lighthouse. It was built in 1899 and called Jeffrey's Hook. Its charm is captured in a children's book entitled *The Little Red Lighthouse and the Great Gray Bridge.*

Outboard Race Day

The Lighthouses along the Hudson were the most popular places to view the old Albany to New York City outboard races held annually for many years. An invitation from a keeper to come out early meant the privilege of seeing the show from the tower—a wonderful vantage point for pictures, plus the thrill of often spotting a boat before others and calling down "here she comes". Of course many treked out to the Lighthouses uninvited to sit on the rocks or deck or to even tie up a boat. And every boat owner, small or large, showed up that day somewhere along the channel to see the first racer through and time him.

The gun started them off at 6 a.m. regardless of weather. Each racer arrived the day before by truck or carrier, and fussed all night with each detail. Racers visited around and swapped stories. These small boats were hydroplanes and not equipped as are the outboards of today.

These races were first held in late April, but in 1927 moved up to Mothers Day in May by the Middle Atlantic Outboard Association when the water was warmer. They were always held on a Sunday. The races stopped at the beginning of World War II. Mr. Hearst donated cash prizes.

The race was a grind as well as a hazard for the 140 miles. In rough weather especially terrible. The tide in certain areas was a big factor; if with the boat, plus a favorable wind, a big asset; if against, each wave was bad, especially if the wind was against the tide. Swells from other crafts could swamp the small boats. Observers, anchored along the channel could be helpful if a spill or breakdown occurred, but often sightseeing craft wove in and out and caused the racers trouble. The casualties

Fred Hildebrandt on Race Day

were often towed into the Lighthouse and tied up, while the drivers were dried out and given coffee; also first aid if necessary. Many had motor trouble but were disqualified if given help in repairs. If they made it through Haverstraw Bay, they were lucky. Sometimes in fog, they got lost and blessed the fog bells on the Lighthouses. The first to get to New York made it before the Day Liner met them; later ones had to risk the swells, and she threw a bad wash.

These races were recently started again with larger boats over the same course, but the thrill is not the same. They are more powerful and better equipped. Two men (although there have been women running this course) who now wear helmets and special jackets, roar by with greater speed. They seldom flip or swamp, and usually all make it to the finish line. In the old days, many started and few arrived.

Now, as they pass the Lighthouses, there is no crowd waiting on them. Those not already torn down have been boarded up since 1954 with "no trespassing" signs. The decks and docks are decaying and there is no place to tie up a boat of any kind. And soon there will be no Lighthouses; just steel towers.

Past And Present

It is amusing, even pathetic, in these days of high prices and waste, to read the logs of the old keepers. Pennies were pinched on supplies and every paintbrush had to be worn down to the handle before a new one was issued. The brass had to be spotless and still the polish carefully hoarded. A brass rail to the tower was rarely touched for fear of finger marking it when an inspector might be due. This called for a keeper to put on his uniform which he was carefully keeping for his burial. Wicks could not be carelessly trimmed and each gill of oil had to be accounted for; no new broom until the old one was down to a stub. Now the military are not so worried. Yet, with all the new aids to navigation and river charts available, many small craft run aground each year, and each year there are hundreds of new pleasure boats. They forget or never bothered to learn that odd numbered black cans lie to port and even numbered nuns to starboard, and the rules of the road are red right returning. Many get confused with this, which should read "returning from the Sea".

LEGENDS

Ferries at Saugerties

Few these days realize the difficulties years ago to cross the Hudson River or even the Esopus Creek. With no bridges or ferries then, the other side was an unknown world to many. Of course, one could walk across in winter, at least, usually, for three months. And some type of raft or dugout was used before row boats. Logs were floated across from upper Saugerties to Clermont, even in the old days of the local Sawyer's Mill. And likely, men with long poles waited for favorable tides and winds to ride them across. Much later, the river Sloops docked passengers at landings.

But the first real river ferry in the Saugerties area, crossed from Brink's property (now Mertens) to Clermont, before 1800, though a crude affair.

Mynders had a rope ferry in 1800 from Stony Point (now the site of the U. S. Coast Guard on the north side of the lower Esopus). This landed at Ferry Street, a busy section even then. William McCaffray also ran a river ferry, horse propelled by a tread mill, in 1800, from the Overbagh Farm on the river, to Tivoli. A horn hung on the pole to call for a crossing.

In 1828, the New York State Session Laws appointed Robert Livingston, John S. Livingston, Peter Outwater and associates, "a Body Corporate Politics", under the name of Red Hook and Saugerties Ferry Company capitalized at $8,000 to operate a ferry, subject to control of Dutchess County Court. This was horse propelled by a treadmill.

Persens Ferry was across the upper Esopus near the present Hill Street-9W bridge. Solomon

Old Airline Ferry at Saugerties

Roosa had earlier built a pontoon bridge across the lower Esopus and in 1829 moved it to the Hill Street site, where it was destroyed in 1830 by a hurricane. A wooden arch bridge was built here in 1839 and destroyed by a freshet the same year and a foot bridge replaced this in 1840. All these were toll bridges. Later Ralph Biglow built a bridge here for $7,000 and sold it in 1851 to the town for $3,000.

Earlier, in 1842 the New York State Sessions Laws had appointed Robert Livingston to grant a permit to John L. Coon to run a ferry from Saugerties Landing to Red Hook for 15 years. But in 1851, they also issued a charter to Messers. John A. Overbaugh, William Bart, and Russell Isacs, to furnish ferry service to Tivoli for 12-1/2 cents a person (in 1853 this was increased to 25 cents).

By 1851 there was a steam ferry boat, the Chelsea, to connect with trains at the newly opened

New Airline Ferry at Saugerties

Ferry "Robert A. Snyder"

Hudson River Railroad at Tivoli. But the dam broke
in 1857, and sank the Chelsea at "Magazine Point",
or "Powder Depot", (now the U. S. Coast Guard).
 Oliver A. Fields in 1859, ran the "Black Maria"
later called the "Fanny Fern", for 25 cents a person.

View of Harbor showing Sheffield Paper Mill, Saugerties, N.Y.

Capt. Fields ran several sloops to the Southern States from his dock near his mansion.

The very popular "Air Line" started in Pennsylvania, as a wooden side wheeler named Kaighn's Point Ferry in 1832. It was an unusual beam type— 73 feet long, 20 feet wide and drew 7 feet of water. It had an octagon pilot house and a rudder only on one end. It sank and was rebuilt and renamed the "Air Line" after the Air Line Ferry Company. Then it came to Saugerties in 1860 after going around Sandy Hook, to avoid the tolls. On its trip north up the Hudson, it is told, she ran into a bad storm and the anchor was thrown over without fastening it. Her crew served so long, they were called the "ancient mariners". The ice sank her in 1866, but she was soon back in operation. The State Legislature allowed them to tow vessels in and out of the Esopus Creek, a busy place those days. The Robert Snyder family owned the Air Line for many years, until returned and dismantled in 1915 in the Rondout Creek, a grave yard for many ships.

There was no ferry locally from 1915 to 1921, when the "Menantic" a larger ship, operated from the South side slip until 1929. She also serviced the trains, at Tivoli; and again no ferry until 1931, when the Hannay Brothers operated a small double ender from the Long Dock to Tivoli. Originally the Queen Mary, it was renamed the Saugerties. It was a short crossing and very popular. Old Capt. Charlie Buckman and his wife, Rose, who lived on the long Dock, assisted with the service and enjoyed visiting with the passengers as they waited. This stopped in 1938 and the ferry was sold to Florida.

Ferry at Saugerties "Ida"

The Tivoli Ferry

And so stopped all ferry service in the Saugerties area. Despite the many river bridges, the ferries are missed for a quick crossing, unless one can induce a cruiser or local boatman to row one over. Dockage is dangerous these days though, even to tie up. Pilings are rotten and wharves have caved in. And ice walking is a thing of the past, with the U. S. Coast Guard keeping the river open for traffic all winter.

Old timers remember the trips; often just a boat ride back and forth with the whole family and waving to the Lighthouse Keeper in passing as he rang the bell; a chance just to see the river.

The Old Wreck

There is an old wreck, about two hundred yards north of our island home, that has a history and a bit of a story. It is completely under water at high tide, but its two hundred foot long timbers and iron pins still show at low water, despite its many years of battering from the ice. Being out of the channel and on a flat, it is no hazard to shipping; but a small outboard or canoe could pass over it at high water and rip the bottom of the craft. So my husband, each spring, wires a new painted marking pole to show its location at high tide. The ice tears this off each winter.

The wreck is the remains of the Saugerties, which burned at her dock in the Esopus Creek in 1903, and was dragged around the lighthouse and grounded on the flat, to burn to the water line. It

Locating the old wreck at high tide

The Saugerties night boat which burned in 1903 to become a shipping hazard

The old wreck at low tide with burned hull exposed

was originally the Shenandoah, brought up from the South for the Saugerties Night Line service, and made many trips back and forth to New York City, with passengers and freight.

Captain Coons of Wappingers Falls came to see us in the 1930's, as it seemed, he used to live on our island long ago, and told us he worked on the Saugerties in the engine room. But he was away at the time she burned and on return was very upset, as he had a personal loss. He had buried a keg of rum in the hold, and immediately on his return, borrowed a rowboat from an old buddy and rowed out to the wreck with shovels to try to salvage his rum. But the hold had settled deep in the soft mud and he had no luck. By now time and nature surely have eliminated his keg of rum. Captain Coons died long ago, but the heavy timbers of the old ship are still solid under water.

Esopus Creek—
Past and Present

Often, as modern cruisers, speedboats and occasionally a sailboat, come in and out of the Esopus Creek, a confluence of the Hudson River at the Saugerties lighthouse, one may wonder if this breed of boatmen ever think of the many different craft that have used these waters in years gone by.

Now they call it the Saugerties Creek; seldom the traditional name, the Esopus, which came from the local Esopus Indians. Now there is no commercial shipping of any kind. Yet only thirty odd years ago, three or four large pleasure boats were berthed here. Then the Saugerties Night Line ran to New York City daily (except when laid up by ice). A steamer left the foot of South Bridge Street each evening and a sister ship arrived back in the early morning, allowing a good twelve hours to do business or visit in the city. Everyone knew the Ida and the Robert Snyder. They carried passengers and produce, and one could have a stateroom or relax on deck and watch the lighted towns go by.

Also tugs brought barges into the creek, loaded with coal or lumber for the paper mills near the dam and they took out blue stone for New York City. No one knows the huge tonnage of stone shipped from the Esopus by Captains Field, Brainerd and Burhans and the Maxwell dock. They supplied sidewalks, curbing, lintels for doors and special cuttings for fancy jobs. For years, a ferry ran back and forth to Tivoli and the shad fishermen waited for the right tide and wind to drift their gill nets out on the Hudson.

The creek has been dredged several times—the last in 1928—and pumps poured the spoil in behind the dykes that were built in 1888 and 1889. A Citizen's Committee built an earlier dyke on the south side, mostly by filling old barges with rock. Before all this, the creek just spread out into the Hudson about 2,000 feet west of where it now enters the river at the end of the dykes at the lighthouse. Not many years ago, a keeper lived here with his family and rang the fog bell when it was soupy; lit the light in the tower and welcomed visitors. This house is now empty, closed, and the light is automatic.

Long before the lighthouse was built in 1868 (there was an earlier small one), wood-burning steamers raced up and down the river, with bets laid on their speed. And before that, sailing sloops were common for commercial travel and wives and sweethearts rowed out on the creek at dusk, to hang lanterns on posts or trees to guide their men home after dark. The larger boys in the family were with Pa on his ship, helping out. The skipper would blow his horn or ring a bell, and from the echo on the high rocky cliff opposite the creek, one would know he had reached Saugerties. Sometimes the echo was distorted in a heavy fog, and it was best to drop the hook. Some sloops had slaves in their cargoes, fleeing north, and it was said Saugerties had its underground railway.

During the Revolutionary War, the British entered the creek and burned all sloops at their docks; and long before Indians paddled in and out for fishing and for access to their village and cornfield nearby. Indians were in these parts thousands of years ago. Artifacts of a primitive people have been found here recently.

How many speedboaters dashing in and out of the Esopus today know or care about those who used to row out and hang the post lantern? Or before that, what lonely brave watched for enemy war canoes?

Heaven at Krum Elbow

The charts of the Lighthouse Service, years ago, listed a flashing light for navigation, on the East shore of the Hudson River at Hyde Park. This was called Greer Point, and on the opposite side of the river, at a sharp bend, it listed Krum Elbow, taken from an old Dutch name.

When Mr. Roosevelt became President of the United States, he wished this changed, claiming Krum Elbow was on his side of the river. His estate bordered along the shore at this point.

The owner of the estate on the western shore, objected strongly to this change, claiming his side was called Krum Elbow for generations, and many agreed with him. But Mr. Roosevelt arranged to have all maps and charts changed and Greer Point was eliminated.

The gentleman across the river was outraged and sold his entire property, and it is said, moved to Canada. The new owner surprisingly was Father Devine who moved in with his followers, called Angels, and he erected a very large sign on the river bank easily seen from across the river, simply painted "Heaven", which is what he called all his various communities throughout the valley. Needless to say, the President was not pleased. It greatly amused the Day Line passengers.

Depth of Focus

I consider this little book "A Depth of Focus". To a dedicated camera fan, this needs no explanation. But nearly everyone these days has a camera of some sort. Many can not change their focus; it stays fixed; others can blur or fade out the distance and sharpen up the close up detail; or in reverse make the distant view more perfect.

I am an old lady and memories of the past are often very sharp. The sloops, the night boats, the pleasure steamers that carried thousands up the river to the mountains, the fishermen's nets and long strings of barges with their families on board; all are gone.

Now our Hudson River is dredged for large tankers and freighters from all foreign ports. And huge cement barges load at plants that have stacks belching out clouds of noxious smoke. Tall towers take the place of our lighthouses, closed and decaying.

Hundreds of small pleasure craft race back and forth, mostly just for the sport of speed or noise. The occasional sailboat is a welcome sight, but has its traffic hazards these days.

So much has been written about our Hudson River—its beauty, history and old estates. Recently the focus has been on its pollution and neglect. I live very close to the water and see its activities—the dredging, the industrial plants (sadly on the shore line instead of behind the hills), and of course its pollution.

People are becoming more concerned now. Even the beautiful sloop, the Clearwater, is alerting us. Maybe our younger generation will do a better job than the old-timers.

From Old Lighthouse Records

Sixty years ago the government sent the following to all lighthouses for first-aid treatment:

Toothache: 2 or 3 drops of creosote on cotton on gums.

After any infectious illness, boil all bedding in one part to 1000, bichloride mercury, 2 or 3 hours.

Dysentery: 2 tablespoons castor oil and 15 drops laudanum.

Cholera Morbus: mustard plaster and 15 drops laudanum.

Scurvy: mouth wash potassium chlorate.

Sore Throat: gargle potassium chlorate.

Coughs: tablet—Brown's mixture.

Erysipelas: dust skin bismuth submitrate.

Arthritis: Bella donna plaster, accute casses 5–10 grains salicylate soda.

Burns: strychnia sulphate—1/4 grain; prick blister
    with clean needle; sprinkle dry boric acid; or
    cover with carron oil.
Frost bite: use snow and rub gently.

    Government list for weekly food supplied for
each man in a lighthouse or on a tender:
3 lbs. pork—7-1/2 cents a lb.
4 lbs. beef—6 cents a lb.
1 lb. flour—4 cents a lb.
1 lb. rice—3 cents a lb.
1/2 lb. raisins—13 cents a lb.
98 ounces—Navy biscuit—4 cents a lb.
14 ounces sugar—8 cents a lb.
1-3/4 ounces tea—80 cents a lb.
4 ounces butter—23 cents a lb.
7 ounces coffee—20 cents a lb.
1-1/2 pints—beans—24 cents a gallon
1/2 pint—molasses—64 cents a gallon
1/2 pint—vinegar—20 cents a gallon
1 peck potatoes—16 cents

To average 20 cents per day per man or weekly—
$1.40 allowed.

A True Conservationist

This is a true story of a man who was one hundred percent for conservation, although I doubt he had ever used the word in his long life. I met him when he was a fairly old man. My husband's work takes him along the Hudson River and he had run across this fellow several times. He suggested that I go to see him and his unusual place. I drove down a back road, rough and narrow to the waters edge, and found him at home. When I praised his remarkable flowers, he thawed out and showed me around his domain and explained his improvements.

Years ago, in his river wanderings, he had come across a swampy area that no one seemed to own as tide water often flooded it. He took it for his own and after many years, with squatter's rights, it was truly his property. "This all came from the river," he said, and he had really salvaged or made all he had. First a few floating pieces of lumber, an old abandoned rowboat, which he soon patched up, further floating odds and ends, and he had a shelter and transportation.

Being a clever jack of all trades, he fished, hunted ducks in season, cut up driftwood for fuel, and each year improved his holdings. Old boats, even chairs and tables can be picked up each spring after high waters. He dug a well, made a fireplace, found a window or a door, and his house grew.

The engineering project that intrigued me most was his canal. Swamp surrounded him at first and with his old boat and a shovel, little by little, he dug a trench from shore to the deeper water, so he could get his boat out to the channel. As he dug, he carried the muck in his boat back to shore, to make land—fertile for a marvelous garden later. This took years to complete. Even then at low tide he could not get out, so he dammed up an area in back of his house to make a pond. Here he put in a gate, a large round steel wheel-like affair. This he could hoist up by ropes to let in the tide water and close to make a fairly large pond. Then he would get in his boat, close to the gate, pull the rope and the rushing water from the pond carried him out to the deeper water. At high tide he would pole his boat back through the canal, and as the pond was now full again, close the gate. Someone gave him rare lotus bulbs which he planted in his pond, and they multiplied and made an unusual display. On his muckland he raised plants to sell and also vegetables. I bought some aster plants, and he went into his workshed and came out with a large roll of wrapping paper, on a commercial rack, to cut off the sheets. He showed me the name printed on the paper—a large firm in Troy, New York—and said, "Found it in the river in a thick carton, so not too wet."

He and his dog Winnie, a sweet little beagle, lived a happy life. His home was really very comfortable when I saw it, with a boat landing for several nice boats, which he rented out to hunters in the fall. Each year he dug in his canal a little or it would fill in or choke with river weeds. Several times he had flooded with unusual tides, but he tied some things to trees, high enough to save them, and dried out everything later. He took it all as a matter of course. His river could do him no harm.

Old Overlook Tales

As a child, I lived in New Rochelle, which was uncrowded then. It was considered dreadful to stay home in the summer. One must go to a resort. My mother became interested, around 1900, in Overlook through our minister, a lover of nature, who had been vacationing at the Overlook Mountain House for years. Each June thereafter, we packed up and spent the summer on the Mountain.

The old hotel was listed as 3,250 ft. above sea level, and had been a famous resort even for visitors from abroad. When we went there, its heyday had passed and it was far from modern. There were three floors of bedrooms, small, bare, no curtains, rugs or extras; just the usual simple bed and bedding, a stand with washbasin, pitcher and slop jar, and an oil lamp. On the second floor was a bath-

The old Hotel

room, but never any water that was even lukewarm. In the attic was a huge storage tank to which water could be pumped up from the reservoir, which was always low.

We started packing in May when two trunks came down from our attic—a big one for clothes and extra blankets (nights were often really cold), and a smaller one for my grandmother, called Gammie by everyone. Her trunk was the most popular object on the mountain all summer. It really contained a little of everything. Overlook was far from a store, and when anything was needed, Gammie went to the trunk. She had first aid necessities, sewing and knitting odds and ends, the kind

A view from the porch

of hard candies that never spoiled, always several
yards of red flannel and cheesecloth, which had
many uses, note papers, pencils, even crayons. To
settle disputes, she always had a dictionary. The
trunk even carried a small alcohol stove, utensils
and cups, which were wonderful for tea or cocoa—
even a hot toddy in the middle of the night. The
huge wood-burning range in the kitchen went out
after supper, and if a hot water bottle was needed,
Gammie was awakened, and her little burner was
on the job. Her trunk was a magician's box for us all.

To get back to our June departure: my brother
and I attended private schools, out early, and late

in opening in the fall, so we had a head start on the resort travel. We took the Hudson River Dayline from 125th St. in New York. My father went with us reluctantly; he always complained about leaving a good bed and good food for roughing it at the Mountain House. Usually my mother and father returned home in two weeks, where the hired girl was left all summer. Her main job during our absence was canning from our huge garden.

Our trip on the boat was a big event. We children had the run of the ship and never sat down until the dinner hour in the main salon. This was a fancy place in those days, with colored waiters and much delay in service, which infuriated my father. Finally, we reached Kingston Point Park with our band on the boat playing and the merry-go-round blaring on shore; here we rushed for seats on the boat train to Hurley. It seemed to take ages for the train to start, but finally we puffed into West Hurley to be met by the stagecoach for Overlook. Tennis rackets, bags, etc., were left to come later with the trunks in the buckboard, which also stopped for mail and groceries in Woodstock. When our stage stopped there, we climbed down and dashed across the street to a shop that had homemade custard ice cream. We never missed this. Then, back to our stage, which by then had added another horse to pull the grade. Further on, the younger crowd got out and walked, often all the way from the cemetery, arriving at the hotel long before the stage. Middle-aged passengers would walk ahead of the horses when the grade was bad, wait two or three thank-you-mams beyond, and then climb in again. My father always rode, although he was not old or feeble—but portly. He said he had paid to ride, and ride he did.

Supper was soon served in the huge bare dining room. Someone rang a hand dinner bell from the porch, and everyone ate before dark, as no light was later available with the exception of a few feeble oil lamps. When the hotel was first built, they made a form of gas, carbide, I believe. Anyway, all the fixtures were still there unused.

After supper the parade on the porch started. Chairs were pushed close to the railing for the few non-walkers, and all others considered it a duty to walk at least a mile. As I remember, this was eighteen double laps around the three sides. Young folks went four or six abreast, singing and keeping step, breaking ranks in passing another group. This went on until after sunset, which everyone had to watch. Truly, the sunsets were gorgeous over Indian Head, and many visitors came for one night just for this display. Some even slept out on the cliff for the sunrise over the valley.

When the moon came up over the Hudson River, with the panorama of the valley below, it was a never forgotten thrill. Someone had a contraption that flashed a light to the nightboats and they would signal back with their huge searchlight sweeping a path over the dark mountain. By this time, dancing was in progress in the very large living room. Pier mirrors, a huge grand piano, a few marble-top tables and straight chairs furnished this room. A carpet covered the whole floor, and we used to sprinkle cornmeal or powdered wax on it to make it slick. As we danced, when the wind blew, this carpet would ripple like waves. Whenever I hear the "Merry Widow Waltz" I can almost see that carpet. Some used to complain that it made them seasick with its up and down motion. There seemed to be someone always handy to play the piano. Some summers, when the hotel was fairly booked up, they hired a couple of college boys to play, one of whom had a musical instrument. I guess it was a board and room arrangement, but they were very popular with the girls.

My father often stayed over the 4th of July, which was a real event, with rockets and flares at night. We would launch huge paper balloons from the cliff, lighting a pad inside that caused the heat to inflate them. As they caught fire easily, six or seven tall boys were usually needed to hold out the paper sides. But when tugging to go, they would take off over the valley, and if the wind was right, would often sail high and far. We would attach addressed tags to them, and frequently got replies from quite a distance. These balloons were surely fire hazards over the mountain growth, but nothing ever happened. After the 4th, my mother usually left with my father and Gammie took over. They would return for Labor Day, if not before.

Meanwhile, we would be busy every day. There was a run-down bowling alley in back of the old cottage near the spring, which had much use in spite of its condition. Also popular was a large billiard room under the hotel living room. There would always be a young married couple to chaperone hikes, which involved trips to Minister's

Face, Echo Lake, Indian Head, and even as far as Big Indian where they had a good bowling alley. We would hike over the back road to Devil's Kitchen and camp out at Young's at the top of the Plattekill Clove. Then down to West Saugerties for a night of square dancing, and back the next day through Woodstock and up the mountain. We carried our own equipment on these treks—each one, some item needed. The boys and men carried the heavy articles, but we each had a walking stick and blanket roll. This consisted of a poncho, spread with a blanket next, in the middle of which a few articles could be laid, and the whole rolled lengthwise. With the ends tied together, it could be slung crosswise over one shoulder; a sweater or jacket could be secured around the hips. Some of the husky boys carried knapsacks. A hot water bottle often took the place of a canteen, but springs were usually located. We would have among us one lantern, one hatchet, a frying pan, a coil of rope, coffee pot and nested tin cups. Food was bought where available, but we always carried coffee, condensed milk, cocoa and canned ham, at least. Sometimes we would buy a good dinner at some boarding house along the way. Nights, we would cut a lean-to and spread out our ponchos. No sleeping bags then. Everyone wore hiking boots, often with hob nails. The girls wore short skirts—slacks were unknown. Rattlesnakes were common in that area, and we skinned many and made belts. One young college boy tried injecting the serum into a frog, and I shudder now to think that I held the frog, and no doctor or phone within miles.

Mead's Boarding House

There was a crude tennis court halfway up on the cliff, and we held tournaments there and down at the court at Mead's. The cliff was the place for a real view. On a clear day you were supposed to see seven states, from the Green and White Mountains to Delaware Water Gap. Seven States Rock was carved with initials, including General Grant's. We grew tired of walking back from here the same way to the hotel, and hacked a path through the woods around to the back road, and on this back to the Mountain House. As I was good with the axe, the boys made a large sign "Ruth's Path to the Hotel" and erected it out on the cliff's end. I was thrilled.

Evenings, when dancing bored—and many older ones did not dance—we played charades, in which all could join. There were many talented people at the hotel, off and on, and the charades often grew into theatrical affairs. Eddie Foy's boys were there all one summer, and they could mimic their father even then. Katherine Tupper, now Mrs. George Marshall, had studied dramatics, and her "Taming of the Shrew" was expert. There were Mr. and Mrs. McEntee of the Ben Great players, and many other gifted people.

A mock trial or mock wedding was fun, and one mock trial that I remember was a riot. We had hiked to Echo Lake, and a young Cuban boy and I had stayed to fish after the others started up the trail. A herd of cattle sometimes grazed through there, and the bulls were mean and chased us this day. We could only climb a tree, and the Cuban boy managed to get up first and then helped pull me to safety. He had a revolver and fired a signal, and the rest returned to our assistance. They ragged him for being first up the tree, and held a mock trial that evening to decide his guilt and penalty for being unchivalrous. He was so confused, in his broken English, that I finally refused to press charges.

When we held a masquerade, Gammie's trunk came into full play, and the costumes were surely original, often very clever. Someone always took a picture with a flash powder. These affairs ended with a Virginia Reel, and then the cellar would be raided for a case of birch beer.

As summer progressed, we all picked huckle-berries by the pailful. In the fall, my father's favorite sport was chestnut gathering. These huge trees were plentiful then. He would sometimes come up late, after the Overlook had closed, and stay with my mother at Mead's, just to gather chestnuts. This was foliage time, a wonderful time for artists, who were flocking to the area by then.

Now these days have gone; cars drive through in a rush; few hike, and most of the old resorts are no more. The old Overlook went down in a blaze of glory, with no fire protection. The cliff path is overgrown and dangerous with snakes. But the view, sometimes with banks of puffy white clouds below, and often with the Seven States visible, is still there and still remembered by many.

Fishing on the Hudson

Back in the early part of the 20th century, Hudson River fishing was a means of "livelihood, as well as a sport." In a house near where I live, a family of thirteen had no other source of income but fishing, except a garden, a few fruit trees, maybe a pig or chicken. Of course, they ate plenty of fish. But with often a haul of 2,000 pounds of carp in their nets, just in one night, at thirteen cents a pound, they could sometimes afford pork chops. Tank trucks came from the cities to keep the fish alive in water until reaching the market for Jewish trade. This is no more, although the carp are still plentiful all summer.

There was all year fishing, starting with pelican in early spring (which they smoked), then herring, shad, sometimes a run of smelts in the nearby creek.

Claude — a Hudson River fisherman

Maybe a sturgeon got in the shad nets, which ruined the net, as they averaged from two to four hundred pounds. These were called "Albany Beef". Their eggs were as high priced as caviar. Later, there were bullheads, eels, a few bass, sunfish and white perch all summer. When ice came, holes could be cut in the creek near the river entrance and white perch or pickeral could be caught. Even a pike net could be put under the ice along the river shore to catch bullheads.

Men came in winter from other towns to ice fish in the lower Esopus. They would sit on boxes and often have a fire on the ice, as they watched several tip-ups at once.

Down river, where there is more open water in winter, striped bass are plentiful still and are caught commercially as well as for sport. The power plants—that draw water and discharge it warm into the river—have been under conservation scrutiny lately, regarding the bass as they spawn there.

In regard to fishing methods used long ago, pelican and shad were netted from early April to late May. The shad only come up here from the sea to spawn. Shad fishing is a tough job on the ebb or flood of the tide, and requires two men to drift the huge nets from a small boat. Few will do this anymore. Also, pollution has ruined the market for some, although the Hudson, from Catskill to a little north of Poughkeepsie, is listed as the cleaned part of the river, and the fish are still there.

Herring was scapped from a rowboat with a small square net attached to a pole that could be lowered and hoisted by a handcrank, as the fish

An unusual photograph of fish spawning holes at low tide
swam into it. Old-timers salted these down in tubs
or crocks for winter use and many a dirt cellar had
a good supply. Some herring were also smoked.

Bullheads, eels and sunnies were caught all
summer on a hook and line. Eels could be caught
from a small boat by bobbing in a fairly shallow
water. A mass of garden worms were tied with a

stout string into a large, squirming ball and hung over the side of the skiff. As an eel, maybe even two at once, grabbed on a long dangling worm, the line was quickly jerked up and the eel dropped off into the boat. Often a fisherman sat leisurely doing this until the bottom of the boat was covered. These had to be kept wet and skinned for market. This is now a lost art, but eels and skinned bullheads used to bring good price if fresh. Some even used wire eel traps, baited with mussels.

These methods continued for years in all seasons, but are now past history. Maybe some day, before too late, the river will be cleaner and fish will be better protected by laws. River traffic will increase and will always handicap commercial fishing.

Our Nautical Highway

We have come a long way from the primitive Indian dugouts of long ago to the huge tankers and freighters now on our Hudson River. Traffic these days is heavy on the one hundred and fifty miles from New York to Albany. Old sailing captains, on their sloops, knew every flat and hazardous rock, and could leisurely enjoy the scenery and even visit local communities as they waited for the tide or the wind.

Now speed and economy prevail. In olden days, ice closed travel; even lighthouse keepers turned out their lights, usually in December to April. The ice was harvested and stored away in huge ice houses. Ice jams piled up and often caused damage.

Watching the traffic float by

Large ships now traveling day and night keep heavy ice from forming in the channel, and the U. S. Coast Guard assist smaller craft when needed. Of course, the bays and coves can have two or three feet of ice, but it is broken due to the swells from large ships and the tide. No more skating or ice boating, except in rare locations along the river.

The channel has been dredged to 32 feet and soon may be even deeper, also widened in many places. Aids to Navigation have it buoyed, lighted and well charted. Many ships still carry a pilot, but some groundings still occur. I see ships of the world pass my door—from Japan, Australia, Philippines, Formosa, and recently two beautiful Russian ships, the first on our river. Also, many others from all over Europe. The Swedish and Norwegian ones usually look immaculate. Many ships fly the Liberian flag, some Panamanian, for financial or labor reasons, often with foreign crews. Some American ships now do this.

Texaco tanker passing under Kingston Bridge

View from bell on top of Saugerties Lighthouse

The local cement travel has displaced the long strings of brick barges, each with their families aboard. One type of cement barge, ocean-going, is electronically controlled and pushed by a huge powerful tug. It can carry 90,000 barrels of cement a load.

The smaller, old barges, often four or five, would string out behind the straining tug. The little shack on each often housed a large family, children, dog, cat, even chickens on the deck. There would be red geraniums or tomato plants in old tubs, and a line of wash flapping in the breeze. Winters, they were tied up at a city dock and the children went to school a couple of months.

These days every Tom, Dick and Harry has a boat of some kind, from a small outboard to an elaborate cruiser. Sailboats are often seen now. One can rent a houseboat, all ready to go, at several places along the river. Owners often do not even live near the river, but keep their boat at a club or marina.

Our old Day Liners now gone, have been replaced by one modern ship that only goes from New York to Bear Mountain. It does turn around at Poughkeepsie, but it cannot land there, due to the condition of the docks. There is one other cruise on the river, from Rhode Island, going through the Hudson to the St. Lawrence and back down the Hudson; usually a twelve day cruise. Mid-western rivers do big business with many cruise ships; possibly because they have less ice in the winter and can run ten months a year. Still, with our history

U. S. Coast Guard "Eastwind" off Saugerties Lighthouse

and scenery, it would seem tourist travel would warrant a trip on the whole river.

The Hudson is now policed. Sheriffs have fast speedboats, and the U. S. Coast Guard have boarding parties to inspect small craft for safety, equipment and pollution checks. Speed is only enforced in certain areas. The large tankers and freighters often travel too fast and can cause bad erosion along the shores. Their heavy swells and pullouts can wash out small docks and damage a beach or stone walls. As we seem to be getting larger ships all the time, this can get worse.

Conservationists are more aware the past few years of our river's potential and beauty, and much is being corrected, although slowly. Phosphates from soap powders and sewage are causing a growth in bays and coves that is harmful to fish and unsightly. In fact, it often closes a bay to small boats.

This surely could be controlled. Many are doing more than their share, some nothing. A balance must be reached between progress and survival of wildlife, even mankind, before too late.

Winter on the Hudson

Few remember the days of the ice harvest, when men, boys and horses worked from dawn until dusk on the Hudson River cutting ice. The huge old icehouses are long gone, and tools the men used are now collector's items; even a cleated horseshoe is rare. Much has been written of these good old days, and many old pictures are still available. All-year river travel and electric refrigerators stopped the ice cutting in the early 1900's. Even labor costs were a factor.

The river is now a commercial waterway, kept open through heavy ice conditions by the U. S. Coast Guard ice breakers, although many big ships can push through without assistance.

With a path of open water and the resulting ice jams, the old days of iceboating, racing sleighs, and even skating, are gone for good. But the ice has a beauty now it never used to have when smooth. At times, the broken patterns of cracked ice, with patches of bright blue water in between, look like an old fashioned crazy quilt. Sometimes it is ridged like an antique washboard; or the broken fragments shine in the sun like hundreds of diamonds, or a sprinkle of sequins.

The ice makes up first in the shallow coves, long before Christmas, with a silvery fringe along the shoreline. Usually by early January the deep water refreezes each night unless travel by the big ships has been heavy. The water, being warmer than the air, steams when a ship goes through; children say, "the river is smoking." Oil tankers and barges haul all winter—loaded going north,

The tall frame lifts the ice to the conveyor. It adjusts to the tide level.

empty going south. Freighters from foreign countries go up empty to the Port of Albany for grain and machinery. Some go north loaded with pulp wood and other supplies, or from the southern ports with molasses.

Usually, modern ships can travel with no trouble, but smaller barges and tugs are often stuck in the ice and must radio to the Coast Guard for help. In very bad conditions, the icebreakers sometimes line up a convoy of several ships, like a parade going by our island. We had a grandstand seat one night as they anchored off our shore and turned their searchlights across an unusual stretch of smooth ice off their side. The crew, bundled in heavy sweaters,

Icebreaker "Eastwind" U.S. Coast Guard

Chester Glunt on ice cake in the early spring

climbed down to the ice with skates and hockey
sticks, and we watched a swift moving hockey game
across the glistening ice.

One winter, a number of large old Spanish
tramps went to Albany for grain and were stuck all
along the river. Men went ashore over the ice and
visited with river families, really an immigration
violation. Several ships took nearly a week to make
it from New York City to Albany, stuck every mile
or so. My husband was a Coast Guard employee
then, and my phone was kept busy with calls from
reporters of all the valley newspapers, where was
such a vessel and what was being done? The Port
of Albany boss would be holding loading crews on
union overtime, and begging for information.

The river in winter can be a field of snow; suddenly a crack will appear, like a winding brook across a meadow. The tide pushes underneath with terrible force, creating tide-rips which were a hazard in the days of ice-cutting or ice-boating. Sometimes it will blow a bubble hole. If a large ship passes, the ice can crack like a pistol shot, or the whole ice field will ripple up and down in waves. Sometimes the water below murmurs or purrs like a kitten; other times it gurgles in rhythm.

Spring break-up is often a time of fear, as it can pile up huge mounds of ice cakes, often three feet thick, if the tide and wind are bad. Or it can go out gradually, with no damage to docks or sea walls. Then we who live along the river know spring is here, as the returning white gulls ride the ice cakes back and forth with the tide, their screeching heard above the honking of the wild geese resting on the flats.

The Tram Way

Years ago we bought a little point of land that juts out in the Hudson River. It is the last stop on a dead end road that was originally built to haul blue stone to the docks on the Esopus Creek. We wanted it for a weekend camp at first, but later built our home there. When we took it over, there was only one other house on the road—an old two story, run down building, where river fishermen lived.

The road was really a tram way, built of heavy bluestone slabs, to keep the wheels of the stone hauling wagons from sinking into the mud or soft ground. This started at the quarries up in the mountains and ran through the town and down to the docks at the creek. It was laid in two tracks just the width of the wheels with the dirt in the

Blue Stone Stockpile

middle. Two horses usually pulled the load. On the down grade, an iron shoe was chained to one rear wheel to drag it as a brake. This held back the wagon and grooved the stone slab in a deep rut on one side. Sometimes just one wheel was chained, but this could wear the wheel rim badly.

Quarry men called these stones Belgian Bridges, although no one now knows why. After the stone road stopped beyond the rubbing mill where stones were sawed and polished, it could be very muddy after a rainy spell. To get a car over to the Point was often difficult. In fact, when we bought this place, an automobile had a problem to travel on the tram way, as the car width sometimes did not fit the stones and it was a bumpy ride.

Later this road was covered with fill and black topped and most of the tram stones were just covered over. A few were salvaged by collectors, if some one could get help to lift and haul them away, as they were very heavy. They made an un-

Hauling Blue Stone on the Tramway

Tramway stones as a stairway step

usual step at a doorway or bumper at the end of a
driveway, but it is sad so many were covered over.
Now the road is heavily traveled, and lined by
houses; even a Coast Guard Station. Few have
ever heard of the tram way or its unusual grooved
stones.

Who Lived Here?

My children often found Indian arrow-heads and odd stones in the soft white-eroding shell from under the soil. Scientists of the University of the State of New York Museum and Science Service heard of this and seemed very interested in my old tin box full of surface finds. They asked permission to dig in our front yard, but my husband said no very emphatically! He feared that rain would erode our banks and that our tree roots would be damaged. After they returned several times, we compromised on several spots if they worked around tree roots and replaced the sod. They only wanted to dig in undisturbed ground anyway; not near our flag pole or sundial.

Men and women came and staked out several five by five foot areas with lines at exact-levels.

Dr. Funk (right) at digging site

After piling up the sod, they took off the dirt in layers with small spoon-type tools, carefully examining each handfull. The lowest level was the oldest. Their finds were tagged and boxed. My husband was sceptical, for to him only a perfect arrow-head seemed worthwhile.

They found under the shallow dirt some pure white mussel shell down to solid rock which is of irregular depth. Indians must have eaten lots of mussels here for years! There are shallow flats around our island, ideal for fishing and digging mussels—called fresh water clams, and they are still there.

They found some broken pottery with marks like etching; many odd pieces of stones and bone fragments, and at one place, a blackened group of round stones.

They seemed pleased with the results. The report of Dr. Robert E. Funk follows:

You will be interested to hear that your site was first occupied by Indians of the Archaic

Dr. Funk and crew at work

period about 2000 B.C.; then by people of the Late Archaic period; possibly by Early Woodland cultures about 1000 B.C.; and finally by the pottery makers of the Middle Woodland period who probably lived there about A.D. 800. In looking at your projectile points again I was surprised to realize that the little reddish brown sidenotched point was made of flint from Staten Island, whereas the big white corner-notched point and the speckled grey ovate knife are composed of flint which was brought from Ohio. So you see that the inhabitants of your island must have done either a lot of traveling or a lot of trading!

The Hudson River Valley Commission printed a brochure of the ten Hudson Archeological Sites and our Rocky Point is listed site No. 5. It is one of the few remaining shell middens along the Hudson. They also state "limited excavation" is permitted; none without permission.

But as I sit on our terrace and look up the river for miles, I wonder who stayed here so long, so many thousand years ago? What did they look like? And where did they come from and go?

Our Island

The Hudson River has a three to four foot tide, twice a day, its time depending on the moon. Tide tables vary due to winds and storms, but usually each tide is forty-five minutes later.

I live on a semi-island surrounded by tidal flats that run a quarter mile to the channel; usually covered by a foot of water at low tide; this drops off abruptly at the channel shelf to sixty feet of water. The flats have a mud surface; some places are hard sand, with a base of very hard gray clay.

Hurricane storms on the ocean push the tide up the river, sometimes six or seven feet above normal, which can flood our garden and cover our causeway—marooning us until the tide drops. But we never have water near our house which is high and dry on a rocky ridge running north and south.

"Glunt's Island" center at left of sand bar
Aerial View

The tide has a normal current of about four to five miles per hour. Oil drums, dead trees, even abandoned duck blinds and such float back and forth sometimes passing our island for days, until the natural fall of the river carries them gradually south, likely to ground on a flat, or just be a menace to traffic. One could really sit in a small boat and drift back and forth slowly down the river.

My son, when young used to take a sandwich and water jug, after checking the wind, and paddle his canoe with the tide flow, until it changed and then turn around and go back with the tide, often going quite a distance. Of course the wind could change this, if against the tide. Then it would be rough going for a small boat. Many years ago, swimmers claiming to swim the whole river, depended on the tide to help them; when it changed, they went ashore and entered the water again when the tide turned. Even an expert swimmer can make little headway against the tide.

The first and third quarter of the moon tides are lower than full moon; called a neap tide, when low, and a spring tide when high. Usually the tide is low at our island as the moon rises over the horizon—which I have regretted as I take night pictures and like the reflection on the water.

I prowl the shoreline and watch the snails and small water life at low tide. Our flats are a mussel bed; not as plentiful now as years ago when the Indians discovered this, but many shells are still found. We are bothered by large snapping turtles, usually in spring. Fishing is only good on an incoming tide; they stop biting when the tide turns. People ask me about this or to launch a boat. One man, who hunts arrow-heads along the shore, calls and asks when the water is out.

In winter, we can walk the flats to the channel, watching for tide rips or blow holes. Often the ice cracks into beautiful patterns. The wind can ripple it in ridges and then freeze it that way.

We have a sun dial on our terrace for which I ordered a special plate; "Time and Tide wait for no Man". And another favorite quotation of mine was written by Ralph Waldo Emerson: "But in the mud and scum of things, there always, always something sings."

We bought our island in 1928, really for the children. My young son had boat fever and that meant, first, a safe mooring for a small boat. My husband is employed by the Coast Guard, so we drove all the byroads along the Hudson River, and finally stumbled on this secluded spot. It was only to be a picnic place for swimming and boating, but much has changed since then.

Years ago, it used to be a real island, about one and one-half acres, rocky and high enough not to flood. Previous owners gradually filled in a narrow causeway over the shallow side to the mainland where originally there had been stepping stones to cross at low tide only. This causeway requires careful driving and many have been the minor accidents, often amusing.

The island is near the west bank of the Hudson, right in back of the Saugerties Lighthouse. Old maps called it Wolf Island; then Coon's Island, as three generations of a Coons family lived here. These men all were river folk who worked on boats, fished or cut ice. Later, each owner called it by his name, but our children chose Rocky Point. It is a sharp upcropping of bluestone with depressions that somehow support large trees of many kinds; one, the oldtimers called Balm of Gilead, grows very tall and is somewhat like a poplar.

When we built our house, in digging for the foundation, we discovered a thick layer of pure white, soft shell. Upon inquiry, and by reading histories of this area, we found it was an old Indian shell mound. Mussels were plentiful in the river, and the Indians ate them and used the shell for wampum. The site seems to have been a lookout, possibly for signal fires, as before the dike and the lighthouse were built, a view could be had north and south for miles. Books say that the Indians hid their canoes in Mynderse Cove behind our island, though unnamed then. But mention is made of it being just north of the Esopus Creek. Finally, a fierce battle was fought in the vicinity across the river. I have found many arrow and spear heads, as well as odd shaped stones that have been used in hot fires.

We have been told that, years ago, our island was used for sad events. Poor folk were left here

Close up of Glunt's "semi-island" in the Hudson River at Saugerties, N.Y.

during the Pest to care for themselves or die. Possibly, this is folklore, not fact. At any rate, it was before 1850 when the Coons lived here.

There is an old wreck directly north of us. The nightboat Saugerties, formally called the Shenandoah, burned in the Esopus Creek in 1903 and was dragged out in the river and onto the flats to settle each year more in the mud. My husband puts a pole and flag marker on it each summer as it is a hazard for small boats when covered at high tide. Old Captain Coons, before he died, came to see us as he was born on this island, and told us his interest in this wreck. He used to work on this ship, but was away when she burned and did not return for awhile. When he did, he borrowed a skiff and rowed out to the wreck, as he claimed he had left a keg of fine rum hidden in the bilge. Although he poked around in the debris and mud, he had no luck, but insisted it was down there — and maybe it is.

Our island has had various tenants. One, a hot-headed commercial fisherman, had a swivel gun mounted on the rocky point, originally, to shoot ducks. It is said that an English gentleman, across the bay, often flew on a high pole the British flag for special events, and this fisherman would shoot it down. The bay is wide and he must have been a good shot.

The nearest neighbor was another family of commercial fishermen, just across the causeway. There were thirteen in this family, and they were unfriendly rivals of the island fisherman. Words over a dog finally caused the feud to boil over, and the island man shot and killed one young fellow and wounded another. At his trial for murder, he claimed self-defense and was acquitted. But he knew he could never safely return to his island, and having no money to pay his lawyer, deeded him the property.

It was from the son of this lawyer that we bought our island, for he was never popular with these neighbors as a result of the trial. We were unaware of any of this, and after the deeds were signed and all matters settled, he advised my husband to get a permit and carry a gun. We were appalled! However, we became good friends with this family, and could have asked for no neighbor more kind or willing to help out in trouble.

When we moved here, these fishermen staked their nets for carp at high tide in the coves on each side of our island. When the tide went out, the fish were trapped in the mud and the men, in boots, threw them into flat-bottom boats and hauled them to their fish pond—a dammed up inlet of the river. Here they kept them alive until a tank truck came from New York, as the market then demanded that they be sold alive. Often, a night's haul in two nets would run as high as two thousand pounds. The price then usually ranged from twelve to sixteen cents a pound. Not a bad night's work. Of course, this involved several men and equipment. These days, live carp are not in much demand.

Shad fishing was also a spring event. Two row boats would drag a net between them at slack water, and the catch, years ago, sold well. Shad are scarcer each year, and it is a tough job; men, these days, pass it up. Herring ran in the spring too. These were scapped with a dip net on a stout pole. Smoked and salted herring were a staple food years ago, and all old timers stored them in barrels or crocks in their dirt cellars. Long ago, sturgeon were plentiful; a 300 to 400 pound fish was not uncommon. Often called Albany beef, it could be used for fertilizer, after the roe was removed and sold at a high price. Seldom now is a sturgeon caught, though there is a smaller type called pelican that can be netted for a short period each spring and is usually smoked. These are always under 25 pounds.

One old fellow, next door to us, was quite a character. He would bob for eels off our point evenings and tell us local history, at the same time that we watched the sunset. Bobbing for eels is now unknown. A large mass of live worms is tied with a string into a loose ball and hung over the side of the rowboat. An eel sucks on the dangling worm and is jerked quickly into the boat with no hook; they just drop off and the bob is again lowered into the water. Often, the bottom of the boat would be filled in an evening. Skinned and packed in baskets, the old fellow had no trouble selling them next morning in the village.

This same old man was very photogenic, and I took his picture one day as he sat on a nail keg with a fish net on a reel in back of him. His whiskers, wrinkles, old buttonless shirt, corncob pipe and visored cap made him look like Popeye, the Sailor. At an art exhibit, a local painter admired the shot and asked if the old man could pose for him. I gave him the name and address, and he made his own arrangements. On the day set, he arrived with a group of art students to sketch the old fellow. They were chagrined to find him shaved, his hair cut, and wearing a boiled shirt and his burial suit, with even a small rose in his buttonhole. Said he wanted to "look purty for his pitcher."

This old family is all gone now, and we bought the property to add to our island home. We loved the location from the start, and with our small modern house, stay through the year. When we first came, our road from the village was a tramway, really rough on a car. This was built for hauling heavy bluestone from the mountain quarries to the river for shipping on barges. Horses pulled the stone wagons, and the mud roadway had two strips of heavy bluestone for the wagon wheels, and the horse walked in between. On the downgrade, an iron shoe was chained to one rear wheel to drag as a brake, and this grooved the stone finally into a deep rut on one side. Most of this tramway is covered up now with a modern road. We salvaged a few of the stones, although it takes two or three men to lift one. Some bluestone were called Belgian Bridges.

This area bordering the Esopus Creek saw much activity years ago. It was the landing for ships, the only means of travel except horseback. Stagecoach roads were almost unknown for years after the sailing sloops were active. Produce, bluestone, even passengers went by ship. At the docks, bluestone slabs were stacked in tiers, and cutters worked on orders of all kinds. A rubbing mill shaped the stone, and a sawing mill, using water power, sawed through the stone, often making ridge

The Glunts with the Lighthouse Flag.

marks. Near our property was a large stone building called the powder depot. Now, all this is gone and there is quite a settlement of houses on this road; none, when we came here.

We have a dead end sign at our causeway, and the uninitiated are sometimes surprised when the road narrows to one way. I came home from the village one summer afternoon to find a car half in the water on its side, and two excited very fat city boarders blaming each other. My way being blocked, I got out of my car and asked what had happened. The fat lady said, "I tell Papa, look at de big boat und ober we go!" I have had my own casualties too. One fall day, I crossed with strong winds blowing the dry leaves across the ruts of the road, and noticed a duck boat tied to a tree at the side. Two hunters were unloading their decoys and gear. I heard them yell as I passed, and stopped as they charged me with heated words. It seemed that they had pushed their two guns up on the road, and with the leaves soon covering them, I not only had run over the barrels but had made regular horseshoe curves in each as they were pressed into the ruts!

Icy nights and fog are the worst on the causeway, and we seldom have callers such evenings. In winter, we can imagine we are in the Arctic. Ice piles around us, and often pushes through our stone sea walls. Ships going through the channel crack the ice like a pistol shot, and the tide gurgles and groans underneath, and heaves it into odd shapes and patterns. I am still a camera fan, and love the ice changes. Often, it breaks into a patchwork quilt pattern; white ice with blue-green water in be-

Chester and Ruth Glunt at home

tween—every day a different picture. Sunsets are gorgeous across the cove; sunrises too. From the government lighthouse in our east bay, the beam of light, on and then off, all night, flashes across our house and the garden path. Moonlight on the river is something never to forget, any season.

Always, we have the unexpected happen. Maybe, a small boat needs help or is aground at low tide. Once, we rescued a downed plane; we took the passengers to town and the crew stayed all night with us, after hanging lanterns on the plane and supplying anchors. Even large ships go aground on our flat, and men come, via small boats, to use our phone; in winter, they get stuck in the ice and walk ashore. I looked out one cold, rough, November day, to see a small kayak near shore with a man slumped over the side. With a boat hook, I pulled him in, soaked and half numb with cold. After hot coffee and drying out, he left by land. But he returned in the spring to complete from here his run of the river in his frail kayak. He seemed amazed that our river could have been so rough in November. It can pick up, and waves often pound us like ocean swells. I can always tell, even at night, when a ship passes by the wash on the rocks. To pass a large ship on the river in a small boat can give one a bounce, if not a spill.

When a fog settles down, the bell on our lighthouse bongs pleasantly, not like the horns on lighthouses on the ocean which blast you out of sleep. We stay put here with our dog, and would live no other place. The grandchildren can come see us. I do not want to miss what can happen right here any day.

Acknowledgments

It is impossible to list all the names of the people who have given me encouragement throughout the years. To all, I give my grateful thanks. I particularly wish to acknowledge the cooperation in the permission to reprint articles and photographs of THE NEW YORK STATE CONSERVATIONIST, NEW YORK FOLKLORE QUARTERLY, SPOTLIGHT, U.S. COAST GUARD NATIONAL ARCHIVES, John Douglas, photographer of the Albany Times Union, and my dear friend Donald C. Ringwald, President of the Steamship Historical Society of America, Inc.

R.R.G.

Picture Credits

Stony Point Light
  Palisades Interstate Park—Korbach
Four Mile Lighthouse
  Mrs. Donald G. Greene
Stuyvesant Lighthouse
  Allen J. Thomas
Coxsackie Lighthouse
  National Archives
William Hoose
  Mrs. William D. Gardner
Christian Hoose
  Mrs. William D. Gardner
Sutomatic Beacon
  John Douglas, Albany Times Union
Buoy
  John Douglas, Albany Times Union
Mulford Ice House
  Maude Mulford

Clearing Ice
    Maude Mulford
Saugerties Boarded Up
    John Douglas, Albany Times Union
Turkey Point Beacon
    John Douglas, Albany Times Union
Dayline
    Morris Rosenfeld
Old Kingston Lighthouse
    Alfred Marquart
Parlor in old Kingston Lighthouse
    Cora Rightmyer
New Kingston Lighthouse being built
    National Archives
New Kingston Lighthouse
    Kingston Freeman
Rockland Lighthouse
    Palisades Interstate Park
Race Day
    Frederick Hildebrandt
Author with Lighthouse Flag
    Lewis Rubenstein
Mr. and Mrs. C.B. Glunt
    Middletown Times-Herald Record

All pictures not listed herein are credited to the Author.

Index

Aids to Navigation
  Automatic beacons, 19
  Indian, 5
  Lamplighters, 5
  Sailing ships, 5
Air Line Ferry Co., 83
Albany, ix, 5, 14, 73, 115
Albany beef (sturgeon), 35, 112, 142
Archeological sites, Hudson River, 134
Artifact, primitive, 91
Athens, N. Y., 8
Balm of Gilead, 138
Bart, William, 81
Bear Mountain, 50, 119
Belgian Bridges (bluestone), 128, 143
Ben Great Players, 108
Bigelow, Ralph, 81
Big Indian, 106
Body corporate politics, 80
Brainerd, Capt., 90

Brink's property (ferry stop), 79
British flag, 140
Buckman, Old Captain Charlie, 83
Buckman, Rose, 83
Burhans, Capt., 90
Canada, 93
Catskill, town of, 112
Churchill, Winston, 45
Clermont, town of, 79
Commerical fishing, 35, 37, 38, 39
Coons, Captain, 88, 140
Coons, John L., 81
Coon's Island, 138
Crum Elbow (Greer Point at Hyde Park), 44
Day Line (Hudson River), 33, 49, 50, 51, 75, 93, 119
  Ships: Alexander Hamilton, 50
           Robert Fulton, 50
Decker, Dr., 58
Delaware Water Gap, 107
Devil's Kitchen, 106
Dickson, John T. (see Dixon), 58

Dixon, John T., 57
Echo Hill, 18
Echo Lake, 106, 108
Emerson, Ralph Waldo, 137
Esopus (Creek), 90, 91, 112
Esopus Creek, 50, 79, 86, 89, 127, 139, 140, 143
Esopus Indians, 89
Father Devine, 93
Ferry Boats
  Black Maria, 82
  Chelsea, 81
  Fanny Fern, 82
  Menantic, 83
  Transport, 57
Ferry Co., Red Hook & Saugerties, 80
Fields, Oliver A., 82
Fields, Captain, 83, 90
Flirtation Walk, 67
Foy, Eddie, 108
Funk, Dr. Robert, 133
George Washington Bridge, 73
Glasco, 24
Great Gray Bridge, 73
Greer Point, 44, 92
Hannay Bros., 83
Hamburg Ice House, 24
Haverstraw Bay, 70, 75
Hearst, Mr., 74
Hill Street – 9W Bridge, 80
Hoose, Christian M. Parslow, 16
Hoose, Emma, 16
Hoose, Frank Lester, 16
Horan, J. J., 57
Hudson Champlain Celebration, 29
Hudson City, 12, 20
Hudson River Conservation Society, 43
Hudson River Lighthouse Station Log (Dec. 1879–Mar. 1908), 55–58
Hudson River Railroad, 82
Hudson River Conservation Society, 43

Hudson River Valley Commission, 44, 134
Humphrey, George R., Jr., 57
Humphrey, George R., 57
Hyde Park, 44, 92
Comanche, ice breaker, 65
Ice harvest, 23
Ice houses, 24
Indian Head, 104, 106
Isacs, Russell, 81
Jeffreys Hook Light, 73
Kaighn's Point Ferry, 83
Kingston, 12
Kingston Point Park, 103
Knickerbocker Ice Co., 24, 56
Krum Elbow, 92
Lighthouse bells, 11
Lighthouse board, 69, 70
Lighthouse keepers:
  Brunner, Ed, 20
  Burke, Mr., 18
  Carlson, H. H., 33
  Fischer, Harold, 33
  Gray, Cyrus L., 33
  Hawk, Conrad, 33
  Hoose, William, 16
  Howard, Mr., 51
  Kerr, John, 54, 55
  Lange, Chief, 51
  LeClerc, Mr., 72
  Lester, Frank, 16
  McAllister, Mr. & Mrs. Ed, 15
  MacDougal, Jerome, 16
  Mace, Mr., 16
  Murdock, 51
  Pastorini, Ed., 32, 33
  Reilly, Mr., 15
  Walker, Thomas, 33
Lighthouse lamps, 9
Lighthouses:
  Coxsackie, 12, 16
  Danskammer, 11
  Esopus Meadows, viii, 12, 53, 57, 64
  Four Mile Point, 8, 13, 18, 20
  Hudson City, 12, 20, 64

Lighthouses (cont.)
Jeffrey's Hook (Little Red Light-
    house), 73
Kingsland Point, 69, 71, 72
Kingston (Rondout), 12, 13, 51
Little Tarrytown, xii
North Hook Beacon Light Sta-
    tion, 58
Rockland Lake, 12, 67, 68, 69,
    70, 72
Saugerties, 12, 29, 33, 43, 50,
    138
Stony Point, 7, 12, 67, 69
Stuyvesant (Upper Kinderhook),
    12, 13, 14, 15
Tarrytown, 12, 71, 72
Lighthouse service, 18, 41, 44, 92
Light List, 67
Livingston, John S., 80
Livingston, Robert, 80, 81
Long Dock, 83
Magazine Point, 82
Marshall, Mrs. George, 108
Maxwell Dock, 90
McCaffray, William, 80
McEntee, Mr. & Mrs., 108
Mertens (Brink's property), 79
Middle Atlantic Outboard Associ-
    ation, 74
Minister's Face, 105
Mountain House, 103, 107
Mulford ice house, 24
Murdock, Mr., 58
Murray, Thomas J., 58
Murrow, Ed, 72
Museum & Science Service,
    N.Y.U., 131
Mynderse Cove, 139
Mynders Rope Ferry, 80
National Archives, 33, 67
National Personal Records, 33
New York, 52, 64, 115, 119, 141
New York Central, 41
New York City, 68, 73, 75, 88, 89,
    90, 125
New Rochelle, 100

New York State Sessions Laws,
    80, 81
Old Lighthouse records, 95
Oliver, Charles W., 58
Outboard races, 73
Overbagh Farm, 80
Overbaugh, John A., 81
Overlook, 101, 103, 109
Overlook Mountain House,
    100
Outwater, Peter, 80
Oyster beds, 68
Paddock's Island, 18
Parslow, Christian M., 16
Pennsylvania, 83
Persens Ferry, 80
Person to Person (television
    show), 72
Plattekill Clove, 106
Pleasure boats:
    Ida, 90
    Robert Snyder, 90
Port of Albany, 124, 125
Poughkeepsie, 112, 119
Powder depot, 82
Queen Mary, 83
Rattlesnake Island, 18
Red Hook, 80
Revolutionary War, 91
Rhinecliff—Kingston Ferry, 51
Rhode Island, 119
Rightmeyer, Cora, 13
Rockland Lake Landing, 68, 69
Rocky Point, 134, 138
Rondout, 12
Rondout Creek, 51, 83
Roosa, Solomon, 81
Roosevelt, Mr., President of U.S.,
    44, 45, 92
Roosevelt, President Franklin D.,
    44
Ruth's Path, 107
St. Lawrence River, 119
Sandy Hook, 83
Saturday Evening Post, 20
Saugerties, The, 88, 140

Saugerties, 12, 29, 33, 44, 50, 85, 91
Saugerties Creek, 89
Saugerties Night Line, 88, 89
Saugerties Station, 32
Saunders, Martin, 57
Sawyer's Mill, 79
Schooner, Mary Atwater, 56
Shenandoah, 88, 140
Sloops:
    Clearwater, 94
    Contrivance, 57
Snyder, Robert, 83
South Bridge Street, 90
State Legislature, 83
State Park, 67
Steamboats:
    Alexander Hamilton, 50
    Albany, 56, 57, 58
    Central Hudson, 57
    City of Kingston, 56
    Drew, 55
    Eagle, 55
    Jacob Leonard, 56
    James W. Baldwin, 56
    L. D. Black, 56
    M. Martin, 55, 57
    Mary Powell, 56, 58
    New York, 56, 57, 58
    Norwich, 56, 58
    Robert Fulton, 50
    Thomas Cornell, 55, 56
Stony Point, 80
Stuyvesant Post Office, 15
Tappan Zee, 73
Tappan Zee Bridge, 72
Tivoli, village of, 50, 80, 81, 83, 90

Treasury Department, 69
Troy, 99
Tug boats:
    A. C. Cheney, 56
    Hercules, 58
    Spaac, M. North, 56
    Rob, 58
    Geo. W. Washburn, 57
Tupper, Katherine, 108
Turkey Point, v, 24, 44, 48
Ulster County, 24
Upper Kinderhook, 12
U. S. L. H. Tenders:
    Daisy, 57
    Gardenia, 58
U. S. Lighthouse Establishment, 5
U. S. Lighthouse Service, 3, 18
U. S. Coast Guard Light List, 13
U. S. Coast Guard, v, 3, 8, 18, 24, 44, 48, 51, 52, 65, 69, 72, 85, 117, 120, 122
Vanderbilt, Charlotte (misspelled Vandervillte), 56
Walker, Thomas, 33
Wappingers Falls, 88
Washington, D. C., 29, 68
Wayne, Mad Anthony, 67
West Indies, 27
West Hurley, 103
West Point, 67
Westchester Historical Society, 72
West Saugerties, 106
Wolf Island, 138
Woodstock, 106
W. P. A., 7
York, Augustus, 57